Praise for Bully i

Dr. Hollis' second book, ***Bully in the Ivory Tower***, is a very sincere description of what often happens in higher education. Hollis is a prolific writer and notable expert in employment issues and workplace bullying. The book is a wake-up call for finding ways to combat bullying in the Academy so that we can effectively reach out to our university community and confirm that it can be more productive. ***Bully in the Ivory Tower*** is a must read for everyone who works in the Academy or is a student at a university.

CLARA WAJNGURT, PH.D.
New York City/Long Island Chapter for Women Leaders
in Higher EducationOffice of Women in Higher Education
American Council on Education

The lessons learned in the recent Sandusky case should signal that a culture of silence in higher education has incredibly damaging effects on an institution and the individuals that work in them. This silence does a disservice to an organization which relies on integrity and ethics as an integral part of its mission. Dr. Hollis' second book, ***Bully in the Ivory Tower***, is akin to her first book by bringing a clear voice to a difficult employment issue while offering viable solutions to recreate a healthy workplace for college staff. Even with my 25+ years' experience in higher education, I find the data in this book to give pause, that higher education has become a surprisingly tough place to work because of the bullying which reportedly runs rampant in our ranks. This book shows that when the lights come down on the college games, homecoming dances, and senior seminars, the personnel who make college the best years of a young person's life are often left isolated in a job, enduring perhaps the worse years of their own lives.

RON G. BROWN, ED.D.
Assistant Vice President, Academic Affairs
Alabama State University

Dr. Leah Hollis brings attention to an important workplace issue in Higher Education that is often not spoken of in public, workplace bullying. This type of destructive behavior can be found at all levels of an organization and affect the morale and success of all staff, faculty and administration in higher education. It is an important read for not only human resource managers in Higher Education but also administrators looking to create an environment of growth and innovation. Toxic work environments lead to high turnover rates resulting in high replacement costs, in not only the cost of the search but in lost productivity. Leah provides visibility to the issue and solid solutions to workplace bullying in *Bully in the Ivory Tower: How Aggression & Incivility Erode American Higher Education.*

VALERIE SUTTON
Director, Career Services Office
Harvard Graduate School of Education

Bully in the Ivory Tower is a surprising but necessary look at the culture in higher education. Over the years, we have watched unfortunately as disrespectful and rude behavior has seeped into our popular culture and personal lives. The results have yielded troubled reactions from those facing bullying by stronger or more popular kids. This book confirms that the behaviors of childhood follow us to professional life. While workplace bullying has taken center stage in many previous studies, this particular book examines the impact on higher education staff and the despair that many feel while working in one of America's highly touted service professions. Dr. Hollis doesn't simply conclude by identifying the problem and the unanticipated yet enormous cost to the academy, she brings forward true solutions for individuals trying to endure a bully, and develops organizational models for executive leadership to stop workplace bullying in higher education.

LINWOOD N. HARRIS, JR.
Former Associate Director Admissions
Carnegie Mellon University

Dr. Hollis's book is a true examination of the need for change in education, in more ways than budgets and tuition costs. *Bully in the Ivory Tower* represents the untold truth of Higher Education. Bullying is a nationwide epidemic usually associated with grammar and secondary school students. Dr. Hollis uncovers a different sector of education that suffers from bullying. The publication depicts how dominant coalitions have ripped away the freedoms that employees deserve the benefit of while at work. This renowned author has once again showcased how the decisions at the executive level need to embrace change. I am overjoyed that I can use the research from this book and apply it to my Human Resources career to ensure we can remove the obstacles and improve institutions and organizational legitimacy across America.

STEVE LEBOON, M. ED, MS.
Society of Human Resource Management,
Lehigh Valley, Diversity Committee

Occasionally, a book disturbs you. In an era of renewed fiscal restraint and cost containment within the academy, the book's timeliness is without question. Refreshingly, the *Bully in the Ivory Tower* does not suggest there are bullies lurking under the bed —Dr. Hollis' book forces one to examine their own professional practice and ideals relating to the associated costs of ignoring bad behavior.

DR. ERIC TURNER
Chief Creative Officer
The HiLT Group

The media today has kept us abreast of the growing level of harassment experienced by children and adolescents in our schools, churches, on sport teams and other social activities. We are quite familiar with corporate power brokers who demonstrate intimidating, aggressive and demeaning behavior. We also do not raise an eyebrow any longer when we hear of another case of sexual and psychological bullying being uncovered within the ranks of the military and law enforcement.

For the first time, this book, *Bully in the Ivory Tower*, pushes open the heavy insulated door to world of higher education. This bright light reveals a workplace with similarly harmful workplace behaviors; but the prevalence in higher education may be more than anyone would have anticipated.

Bully in the Ivory Tower provides a ground breaking collection of insider accounts depicting a wide range of bullying infractions, frequency, duration and the weak kneed response by universities across the nation to these toxic workplace offenses. Does the protected, highly educated elitist environment of idyllic college campuses provide a more natural or perhaps permissive environment for workplace bullies to thrive and grow? Dr. Hollis data suggests that may very well be the case.

Working in higher education administration for more than 22 years, I was not surprised to read of the documented existence of bullying and harassment in my own backyard, but I was, startled by the extent, frequency and the far reaching negative, financial and emotional consequences to the victims; the subsequent domino effect on students, the college/university community at large – faculty, administrators, donors, alumni and ultimately, to those who support these educational institutions........the taxpayers.

Bully in the Ivory Tower will irrevocably change your perception and awareness of the destructive behavior within the closely guarded walls (sometimes even ivy covered) of the higher education workplace. What should be done? Like any problem solving exercise it begins with the recognition that a problem exists. Could *Bully in the Ivory Tower* be the bellwether of institutional change? Maybe, if it could only find its way to the night stands of higher educational professionals and their HR colleagues across the nation.

PAULA K. VAN RIPER–MSW
Assistant Dean Academic Services
Rutgers University

The epidemic of bullying in the United States is beyond disturbing and most people associate it with k-12 students. Dr. Leah Hollis has highlighted this disturbing trend in higher education regarding bullying. Her study has highlighted its prevalence across the organizational structures of higher education. How disturbing is it that the same individuals promoting social justice to college students are bullying each other? Social justice is supposed to instill the virtue that guides us in creating organized human interactions. Dr. Hollis has bravely addressed the behind the scenes incivility which many times evolves from higher education leadership. This book is essential for anyone wondering where bullying exists and how it seems to be so ingrained even in higher education.

CASSANDRA KAUFFMAN
Graduate / Professional Studies Offsite Leadership Coordinator
Cabrini College

Bully
in the
Ivory
Tower

PATRICIABERKLY LLC

Bully
in the
Ivory Tower

How Aggression & Incivility Erode
American Higher Education

LEAH P. HOLLIS, ED.D.

Bully in the Ivory Tower:
How Aggression & Incivility Erode American Higher Education

Published by Hollis, L. P.

Library of Congress Control Number: 2012952244

ISBN: 978-0-9884782-2-0 (Paperback)
ISBN: 978-0-9884782-1-3 (eBook MOBI)
ISBN: 978-0-9884782-0-6 (eBook ePUB)

Patricia Berkly LLC is at www.diversitytrainingconsultants.com

This publication is designed to provide general information relative to the subject matter covered. It is sold with the understanding that the publisher is not engaged in rendering legal or other professional advice. If legal advice or other expert assistance is required, the services of a competent professional should be sought for specific services.

Library of Congress Cataloging-in-publication data is available from the publisher. If you require an alternative version of this publication please contact the publisher.

Patriciaberkly books are a registered trademark.

Table of Contents

Thank You

Praises be to God, from which all things happen. I remain most appreciative of all those who have inspired me to write on this tough topic. Thanks Dr. Tzipora Katz for her technical wizardry. Thank you as well to Dr. Clara Wajngurt for your focused determination which remains an inspiration to me. I am most appreciative of those who beta tested the instrument and lent their insight in the qualitative and quantitative segments. Thanks Eric for your assistance.

Thanks to my brother, Robert, my mom, Dr. Clea, and cousin, Andrew who always tell me to take that next jump at the moon. And thanks to my business partner, Dr. Jeffrey Holmes who is always telling me to "keep it pushing" for that next level of success.

Foreword

Bully in the Ivory Tower:
How Aggression and Incivility Erode American Higher Education

As a former affirmative action director in the University of Pittsburgh System who serves on the graduate leadership faculty at other universities, I find that Leah Hollis' study, titled *Bully in the Ivory Tower: How Aggression & Incivility Erode Higher Education,* brings vivid memories of many episodes of bullying before it was labeled as a cancer in the workplace.

Early in my career in the public schools of Ohio and Pennsylvania, we often talked in the teachers' lounge about the bullies in our classrooms and on the playground. Where were these bullies headed? As educators, we should have comprehended that if these bullies were not taught civility through basic education, they could become our supervisors to bully us in the workplace. It is the bullying we came to accept in our youth that has generated the growth of this costly, disruptive bullying leadership style. Therefore, it is necessary for administrators in our ivory tower culture to identify and eradicate, or at least reduce, the occurrences of bullying.

Our concept of bullying has changed over time. We have been

desensitized to accept the "little boy bullies" with the expression "they're just being boys." Consequently, there is a cultural lag between the current bullying behavior in the workplace and the origin of this aggressive behavior on the playground. The word bully originated in the Dutch culture meaning lover; it has evolved to mean overbearing, overtly aggressive, arrogant, and loud—the henchman and even the pimp. Personally, I can see the origin of word as lover. Little boys are lovable, before they become bullies. At first it was a masculine term; with the women's movement pushing for legislation for equality, women have been granted equality with their share of female bullies in the Ivory Tower.

L. Hollis coined a term, bullrassment, in this study which specifically reflects on the intersection of harassment and bullying. The title also reflects on the days when I served as an affirmative action officer. My responsibilities included dealing with harassment. Harassment was defined as aggressive, negative physical action against employees in the protected classes of race, color, religion, and sex. In essence, perpetrators used this power play over those who were perceived as being less fortunate. Federal laws were ratified to deal with these types of hostility to reduce erosion of protected classes in the workplace. As I sat in my affirmative action seat, the expansion of the protected classes swiftly changed; I saw federal legislation for disability and for sexual harassment. I administered sexual harassment and ADA awareness training for faculty, staff, and students. My office was flooded with concerns of individual rights in higher education. Bullrassment is a term long overdue that captures what happens to faculty and staff who are harassed outside the Title VII protection of civil rights legislation.

Bullying can be vicarious and the victim encounters psychological harassment that may be more damaging. I watched the secretary of a president storm into a vice president's office in a loud, crude manner. She held several loose sheets in her hand and slammed the papers down on the desk in front of the vice president during a conference with me. In the stormy manner the secretary had entered the office; she stated that the president wanted this report before he left for the day. After she turned on her three-inch heels and left the office, the vice president looked up and apologized to me, stating that the secretary was just carrying out the president's directive. The secretary had been empowered by the president, who was a bully, to vicariously bully subordinates of the president. The victim, the vice president, understood the dynamics, and felt the embarrassment and harassment. My conference with the vice president was rescheduled and the vice president completed the report and left for the day. Even vicarious bullying has a psychological impact on employees. In this incident, four employees were directly, psychologically affected by the vicarious bullying. How did the secretary, the vicarious bully, really feel about her behavior an hour later or even the next day? The vice president's secretary left on the heels of the bully, like Paul Revere, but taking a "day walk" instead of a "night ride," announcing, "The bully is coming." Faculty and staff were once again alerted and whispered that they could not wait until the president turned on his secretary or better yet, found another job. Some were even counting their days to early retirement. The whole campus felt the emotional and psychological stress of this encounter, which was one in a series of vicarious bullying events. Another employee, who witnessed the secretary's horrid treatment of the vice president, was psychologically affected, and went from office to office talking about the incident. The vice president, psychologically affected by the bullying, was not in an intellectual state of mind, and completed the report with several errors, then isolated himself to regroup. The report had to be redone. This single vicarious bullying incident triggered much psychological pain and loss of much time on task of the entire campus. As this study will show, there was a fiscal loss as well, as the salary assigned to the professional hours of all four people were lost for the afternoon, as a result of the bullying.

If administration is using a bully style of management, that administrator is literally syphoning off the campus' vital human resources through incivility. As I often think of the aforementioned incident, I think of the lead administrator as a thief. When we analyze how many employees were affected by bullrassment, it is costly and non- productive and the leadership style is questionable. The data collected in this study justifies the term bullrassment that should bring attention to another form of harassment that demands ratification of Federal regulation or legislation.

Dr. Clea Patrick Hollis
Former Assistant to the President/
Director of Affirmative Action
University of Pittsburgh, Johnstown Campus

Introduction

Reflecting on workplace bullying can bring several clichés to mind that are actually applicable to the incivility phenomenon rife in our working organizations. Regardless of the field, institution, or application, workplace bullying is human behavior gone awry with the abuse of power. In a society where so many things seem to be out of control, bullying for the perpetrator can be that irrational attempt to regain some degree of control by controlling someone else.

Cliché #1: "Everything I needed to know I learned in kindergarten"

From a young age, people throughout history have learned to negotiate stress, frustration, and apprehension. In some cases, people learn aggression and control as youngsters and then they are rewarded for such behavior. Aggression learned at a young age from mentors, teachers, and leaders morphs into behavior that may be carried through to the workplace. Whether in sports, finance, or creative endeavors, people model what they see. Aggression begets aggression.

Cliché #2: "What goes around comes around"

Akin to the first cliché, bullying is learned behavior. Someone who has been abused at work or home, who has been the target of bullying or witnessed a bully receive accolades instead of admonishment, may adopt those aggressive behaviors, seeking the same accolades. And the bully will continue those abusive behaviors until checked. The unfortu-nate truth is that those who bully others were typically once the target of bullying themselves. Those who were abused as kids, or witnessed domestic violence, learn how to bully. Kids who were rewarded for aggressive competition can emerge as bullies. Even those who see a suc-cessfully bullying boss early in their careers, learn that bullies succeed. It is the cycle of incivility, going around and coming around.

Cliché #3: "The ostrich puts his head in the sand"

Many times organizations try to ignore the situation, hoping that the bully will go away. Targets often suffer in denial or are slow to report the problem. However, ignoring the problem or putting one's head in the sand only emboldens a bully who finds success in controlling oth-ers through incivility. Bullies are emboldened when their behavior is unchecked. Just like the ostrich that puts his head in the sand thinking the whole body is hidden, the organization with its head in the sand regarding bullying still leaves a large problem silently apparent.

"The stubborn truth" Dr. Julianne Malveaux, June, 2012

As there is no cliché about the wisdom of Dr. Malveaux, her insight on the human condition is applicable to workplace bullying. At the 38th national meeting for the American Association for Affirmative Action, Dr. Julianne Malveaux, former president of Bennett College offered a keynote at the First Day Luncheon. She referred to a "stubborn truth" when reflecting on equality in America. American society is changing;

the demographics are changing. Those formerly on the margins are moving to the front page. While her comments were about the "stubborn truth" regarding societal changes of human relations in America, that truth also applies to the civility that workers do (or do not) show each other. Whether the term is harassment, discrimination, abuse, assault, or bullying, the truth is that incivility and aggression in any form erode the human condition. Stress is a killer; hence, incivility in the workplace can have health consequences for workers and even for the aggressor, who often operates from stress as a motivating factor to control and abuse others. With EEOC complaints at an all-time high in 2011, over 36% of complaints stem from retaliation, a "payback" tactic from bosses. These retaliatory practices and other aggression cost organizations billions of dollars, not only in legal fees, but also in turnover and disengaged employees.

The stubborn truth, in one of the most precarious situations in global economic history, is that individuals and organizations can ill afford to put incivility in the budget. The cost in human capital and the loss of innovation and creativity are incalculable, not to mention the costs of turnovers, complaints, and employee disengagement. To that end, this study, and others like it, strives to chip away at what Malveaux calls that stubborn truth persisting in the everyday of the human condition.

Chapter One

From Homeroom to the Boardroom

Bullying was once thought of as that childhood rite of passage, something endured on the playground. However, bullying, which is pervasive, escalating hostility, and berating and mistreatment on the job can make any organization a toxic workplace environment. Bullying is similar to harassment, making the subject the target of demeaning and damaging behavior. In comparison, harassment is when the target is from a protected class (gender, race, religion, national origin, or disability) while bullying is a class free assault on the target.

The former is illegal under the Title VII Civil Rights laws; the latter, bullying, is still legal in the United States.

Since 1990, a few studies have been conducted which reflect on workplace bullying. Namie and Namie of the Workplace Bullying Institute studied 7,740 adults nationally in 2007 and reported that 37% of American workers have faced bullying on the job. Women are more likely to be the target of bullying and female targets tend to quit their jobs 45% of the time. Further, when employers are made aware of the bullying, 62% of the time the situation escalates for the target or nothing happens (Namie & Namie, 2009). The disengagement and turnover caused by bullying costs American corporations over an estimated $64 billion a year.

Further, there are several studies that examine bullying characteristics in our secondary schools. Of late, tragic stories have come forth about students who have reached out for help to stop bullying at school. Students with an alternative lifestyle, overweight, or from a different faith, tend to be the targets of schoolyard bullying. Some children have lost hope and, tragically, taken their own lives for relief. The response has been to pass particularly stringent anti-bullying laws in education, with New Jersey having the toughest anti-bullying K–12 laws in the country.

This discussion, however, whether about workplace bullying, or schoolyard bullying, misses the problem in higher education. The Ivory Tower is supposed to be a bastion of intellect and enlightenment, showing the way to the American Dream via upward mobility through education. However, if the higher education sector is a subset of American culture, it would seem the shadows of bullying would fall even here. Further, the structure of higher education is dissimilar from corporate structures given its tenure-track system, its reliance on elite scholarship, and other elements that philosophically might not be tied to quarterly balance sheets. Consequently, bullying in higher education administration manifests in ways not examined by previous studies. The result of a disengaged higher education staff or faculty could have a direct impact on the academy's functions of enrollment, scholarship, and advancement. Further, bullying in higher education administration has a direct impact on the cultivation of American competition on the global stage. Bullying in higher education administration turns the focus for its employees from developing critical thinking and intellectually trained graduates to withstanding the day-to-day emotional black eye on campus at the hands of a bullying boss.

Arguably, the casualties of this bullying are not just the immediate target, staff, or faculty, but the students. Imagine teaching a class after being bullied by colleagues or the campus dean. The emotional capital required to connect with students has been spent on defending against the bully, leaving precious little enthusiasm for the students in class. Student services administrators need to be focused and engaged to advise students, guide students, and serve students, especially as many students come to campus with previously identified chronic psychological and social issues themselves. If the bullied student service administrator has also spent his or her emotional capital surviving a toxic work environment, there is potentially no energy to invest in students. Many higher education staff members have commented on the disappointment they endure when realizing that bullying has invaded their departments. Some of these colleagues admit they just don't have the creative commitment for a new project, refreshing ideas, and student engagement. They are spent emotionally while trying to make it through another disrespectful day in the academy.

While bullying is still legal, it is clearly destructive. Higher education, like many other sectors, suffers with bullying practices among staff members and will continue to endure such without proper policies and professional development designed to prevent bullying and hostility. Incivility in the academy doesn't just affect university employees; it has a direct effect on the next generation of students.

American higher education is already under fire regarding its production of viable scientific graduates. The United States ranks tenth in the 2012 Global Innovation Index of 141 nations which were assessed on business sophistication, human and capital research, and knowledge and technology outputs. While the United States ranks second in enrollment for college students, it ranks seventy-fourth in students who graduate with science or engineering degrees (Tomassini, 2012). When these data are examined within the context of a potentially toxic work environment, the urgency to address this problem emerges. Leadership should note that making strides in educational advancement doesn't occur when staff is engaged in the emotional labor required to survive hostility on the job, instead of focusing on enhancing the United States' global rankings in post-secondary education.

Working Definitions

For the purpose of this study, please note the following working definitions:

Bullying: Bullying means harassing, offending, socially excluding someone, or negatively affecting someone's work tasks. This behavior occurs repeatedly and regularly over a period of time about six months. With the escalating process, the person confronted ends up in an inferior position and becomes the target of systematic negative social acts. (Einarsen, Hoek, Zapf,& Cooper, 2003, p. 22).

Vicarious Bullying: Vicarious bullying is a definition coined for this study. Often a leader or manager empowers a secretary, assistant, or fellow staffer to wield his or her power. While this manager is not directly showing aggression, his/her power is extended through an appointed subordinate.

Harassment: Harassment is unwelcome conduct that is based on race, color, religion, sex (including pregnancy), national origin, age (40 or older), disability, or genetic information. Harassment becomes unlawful where 1) enduring the offensive conduct becomes a condition of continued employment, or 2) the conduct is severe or pervasive enough to create a work environment that a reasonable person would consider intimidating, hostile, or abusive (EEOC, 2012).

The Problem of Bullying in American Higher Education Administration

The Namie & Namie 2009 study quantifies the occurrence of workplace bullying across the United States, yet apparently focuses on the corporate sector. Other studies reflect on workplace bullying in Europe (Constanti, 2004; Deholm, 2011; Hunt, 2008; Keashly, 2005). Statistics from the European Agency for Safety and Health (2000) report that 9% of workers, or 12 million people, report being the subject of workplace bullying. In 2005, the EU-OSHA reported that as many of 12–15% of employees are facing workplace bullying. American statistics reflect that close to 37% of workers, or 54 million people, experience workplace bullying in their lifetime, costing some $64 billion annually (Namie and Namie, 2009). The UK reported that one in four people in the workplace are affected by bullying, with 37% of managers reporting they don't have proper management training to defend against bullying in the organization (HR & Diversity, 2010). EU-OSHA (2002) reported that €20 billion are lost annually in dealing with work-related stress.

Studies that focus on workplace bullying in higher education focus on faculty dynamics (Davenport, 1999; Query, 2010; Thomson, 2010). Instances of mobbing and aggression have been documented as part of a tenure-track structure. Therefore, a gap in the literature exists in documenting the occurrence of workplace bullying in higher education administration. Further, the cost of workplace bullying specifically applied to higher education administration has not been examined. In turn, the goal of this mixed-methods study is to quantify the rate of workplace bullying specifically in higher education administration, examine the manifestation of bullying when applied to higher education administration, and develop a model of intervention to limit the problem specifically in higher education administration.

Supervisors and managers from many sectors reflect on leadership styles to engage employees for competitive productivity and innovative problem solving. While transformational and charismatic leadership styles might be particularly alluring, the presence of workplace bullying can erode the positive morale and progress made by transformational or other leadership styles. If bullying extends past the legal threshold of emotional distress or Title VII complaints, the organization could face legal action because of bullying behaviors of their managers. This research intends to collect empirical data regarding workplace bullying in higher education administration and explore potential solutions as they apply specifically to that arena. In turn, leaders, regardless of leadership style, may take these findings to cultivate a healthy workplace in higher education.

How is this study different?

Several studies which are mentioned throughout this book have been conducted to examine the proliferation of workplace bullying since 1990. Many studies examine the corporate sector, European trends, and occurrences specifically on the front lines among support staff or faculty ranks. This study examines workplace bullying throughout the varied administrative sectors in a higher educational institution. Unlike previous studies, this examination specifically considers the cross-section of higher education including admissions, financial aid, development, information services, human resources, student services, academic services, and athletics.

Further, this study considers the organizational level in higher education. As power is a central element to workplace bullying, this study collects data within the power dynamics throughout the organization structures of entry level staff, middle management, deans, directors, and executive levels at four-year institutions. As the landscape of higher education becomes increasingly diverse in the midst of America's significant demographic shift, the data collection regarding higher education will consider the educational level, the organizational status, and the race, age, gender, and sexual orientation of the bullied targets.

Lastly, the data collection includes information on the impact of workplace bullying on specific segments of a four-year institution. Findings will report on the cost to an institution in turnover, along with potential compromised services to students, external constituents, and the general challenge to the university's overall academic mission.

The purpose, then, of this study is to develop new information for higher education leaders who must strive in the midst of changing demographics and fiscal landscapes. New models for leadership can quell workplace bullying to create a more engaged and productive higher education workforce during a time when the higher education sectors continue to face budget cuts and shortfalls. While the focus of this study examines four-year colleges and universities, the findings may be generalizable to two-year schools, career colleges, certificate programs, and proprietary schools at the higher education level.

What is the extent of bullying in American Higher Education?

Several studies have examined workplace bullying in the private and corporate sectors with either qualitative or quantitative methods. Quine (1999) remarked that qualitative approaches tend to be individualistic, focusing on the personal pain a target feels on the receiving end of bullying. In such studies, the dynamics of power and victimization are the subjects. There are statistical approaches that reflect on the differences in the target pool along racial, gender, and generational lines. Other studies have quantified the organizational risk involved in harboring a bully. Once personal pain and disengagement is distilled through a fiscal lens of salary and sick time, Namie and Namie, and a host of European researchers have been able to put a dollar amount on this aggressive behavior.

In a more recent study, Thomas, from the University of Southampton, states, "...quantitative and qualitative paradigms would be necessary as statistics alone could not adequately explain the complex and diverse experiences associated with the social phenomenon of bullying" (Thomas, 2005, p. 277). The field of research on workplace bullying does offer a diversity of findings and perspectives, yet all point to the fact that workplace bullying is destructive on a personal and organizational level. However, despite the growing interest in workplace bullying, there is a dearth of information on workplace bullying in American higher education administration. "Although much research has been done on workplace aggression and bullying over the last two decades, academics have paid relatively little attention to bullying in their own institutions" (Keashley and Neuman, 2010, p. 48).

Research Method for Bully in the Ivory Tower

In an effort to examine workplace bullying dynamics in higher education administration, a thirty-five-question survey was developed. The population comprises faculty and administrators in 175 four-year American colleges and universities. The institutions include liberal arts colleges, Research I institutions, Ivy League universities, historically black colleges, state universities, and large private universities. The commonality in this cross-section of colleges and universities is the baccalaureate degree. Over 3200 participants were asked to complete the survey.

In addition, this researcher has conducted several qualitative interviews with higher education professionals including financial aid, admissions, development, athletics, human resources, and student services personnel. By using descriptive statistics and themes emerging from qualitative inquiry, this study will also yield theories about why workplace bullying is occurring in higher education specifically. Further, an intervention model will be developed to offer solutions to leadership managing the ill effects of workplace bullying in higher education administration. Future studies may build on these findings to isolate an independent variable for in-depth statistical analysis.

Research questions for the quantitative portion:

1. What is the extent of workplace bullying in American higher education administration?
2. Which groups (race, gender, organization level, or education) are experiencing workplace bullying?
3. What is the cost of workplace bullying specifically to higher education administration?

Research questions for qualitative portion:

1. How are targets reacting to workplace bullying in higher education administration?
2. How do higher education managers deal with a bully whom they supervise?

3. What are the effects of witnessing bullying in higher education administration?

Theoretical Frame of Emotional Labor

Hochschild (2003) reflects on the emotional labor that front-line staff members practice when they must maintain professional composure while withstanding emotional distress. Often the target of a bully, in any environment, must manage the emotional abuse, and then find a way to reclaim professional composure.

In higher education, staff members must exert emotional labor to compose themselves after a bullying incident for them to serve students, faculty, and parents. Those dealing with external clients, for example donors, prospective students, and external colleagues, would also exert emotional labor to remain composed despite emotional distress experienced through bullying.

Constanti and Gibbs (2004) examine emotional labor and its application to higher education as service organizations. Such organizations should contemplate the "customer/provider interface, as a means to gain competitive advantage..." (p. 243). Continuing to build on Hochschild, they consider the emotional labor required of front line staff that ". . . has to either conceal or manage actual feelings for the benefit of a successful service delivery..." (p. 243). Further, [they] "argue that teaching staff in higher education are expected to perform emotional labour in order to achieve the dual outcomes of customer (i.e., student) satisfaction and profit for the management" (p. 43).

Arlie Hochschild's groundbreaking work *The Managed Heart* (2003) opens with the notion that employees "sell our personalities" in the course of the workday and engage in "a seriously self-estranging process that is increasingly common among workers in advanced capitalist systems" (p. ix). An employee's temperament is not just a preference, but a requirement, and almost a condition to maintain employment. Similarly, often withstanding bullying is a requirement of employment when the boss is the perpetrator. Enduring such abuse while remaining composed for students requires emotional labor.

One of Hochschild's scenarios considers the Winn Dixie example, which promises civility to customers, promising that a smile is part of the uniform. Regardless of the customer's behavior, agitation, or aggravation, the customer is in the power position. From this power position, the customer has the privilege and almost the right to act in any manner, yet still expects civility and compliance in return from Winn Dixie employees.

The Winn Dixie emotional labor application is ever present in colleges and universities. Staff is often coached to bring that smile to work, regardless of internal emotional strife. Whether dealing with an abrupt parent, unruly colleagues, or even students who act out and act up with foul language and behavior, that employee smile remains a part of the post-secondary uniform, signifying compliance with expectations for exemplary customer service. Yet this same smile suppresses the employees' true feeling of wanting to reply or even just avoid the uncivil situation.

Several organizations have expectations for civility despite the treatment those staff receive when offering service with a smile. Often, such rules, which implicitly suppress anxiety and feelings of the staff, are established by internal power structures.

> When rules about how to feel and how to express feelings are set by management, when workers have weaker rights to courtesy than customers do, when deep and surface acting are forms of labor to be sold and when the private capacity for empathy and warmth are put to corporate uses, what happens to the way a person relates to her feelings or to her face?... Display is what is sold... as enlightened management realizes, a separation of display and feelings is hard to keep up over long period of time (Hochschild, pp. 89-90).

Emotional labor is a requirement; courtesy is mandated in higher education for internal and external patrons despite staff predilections. Consequently, in the face of stress and change, service providers must always strive to connect with students from different backgrounds and values that at times are incongruent with the university culture. Staff must also serve managers and supervisors who may shed the cloak of respect and civility once students or external university staff members have left the building. From seemingly emotional neutrality, the staff goal is to continuously strive for benign acquiescence to professional etiquette at all costs, spending emotional energy to form connections despite their own personal biases, tendencies, and anxieties.

Interestingly, Hochschild, Constanti, and Gibbs focus on the staff exerting the emotional labor in connecting with that front line of customers. In the case of higher education, the application would consider the administrators' relationship with students, internal staff, and external clients. Higher education relies on these internal and external relationships. Yet, regardless of the campus climate, staff success comes from building and maintaining these relationships. This requires energy and composure which can be compromised by bullying behavior.

The maintenance of composure is not only required for external clients and customers like parents, students, and donors; it is required for internal constituencies as well. Higher education has a distinct hierarchical structure which embodies academic rigor and the validation of expertise. Whether one works in the academic and faculty side of the house, external affairs, or student services, the highly credentialed experts are the managers who set the rules for comportment. Hence, the emotional labor exerted to maintain internal relationships in the academy can be even more intense than that required to maintain external relationships. Those in the lower positions of power must continue to put on that smile as part of the uniform and comply with directives, regardless of the manner in which such directives are given. Despite the feelings, emotions, and preferences of the employees, the power structure sets the rules for emotional management.

Within this context, there is the possibility that the power structure is governed by a bully. An aggressive and belittling power structure will undoubtedly require staff to maintain composure despite heightened levels of stress. While these aforementioned studies reflect on the emotional labor in connecting with front-line parties such as students, this study will consider the effort employees need to sustain employment within an ego-driven power structure of higher education.

Within this framework, an additional caveat exists. Those who are not in the power position are implicitly expected to play by the rules set by their employers. In higher education, everyone has an employer. Front-line employees are in the most vulnerable position, which is consistent with other statistics documenting that rank-and-file employees are targets of bullying 55% of the time. Assistant deans are accountable to deans or vice presidents. Deans and directors have provosts. Junior faculty members are at the whim of department chairs and academic deans until the point of tenure. Even the president's cabinet and the president answer to a board of trustees. Any of these structures, if infused with incivility and hostility, will place the subordinate figure in a position to exert emotional labor to maintain composure employment in the academy.

"The mission, if you choose to accept it"

A cursory look at university mission statements illustrates the expectations for staff working in higher education. These three mission statements below were randomly chosen from three types of four-year institutions and not an indication of whether these specific institutions are inconsistent with their own stated goals. Other vision and mission statements are consistent with this type of language, which embraces creativity, innovation, diversity, collaboration, and justice. Whether such mission statements emerge from higher education, the corporate sector, or the public sector, this language requires implicit civility, or at least the *appearance* of civility, to maintain such values.

Cornell University reflects on "...collaborative and innovative culture..." requiring staff and managers alike to work together to create better service for students and external constituents. At the University of Minnesota, "...responsibility, integrity, and cooperation that provide an atmosphere of mutual respect..." sets the tone. The University of San Francisco offers a "...diverse, socially responsible learning community of high quality scholarship and academic rigor sustained by a faith that does justice..."

Cornell University Vision

> Cornell aspires to be the exemplary comprehensive research university for the twenty-first century on the basis of our distinctive status as a private university with a formal public mission. Faculty, staff, and students will thrive at Cornell because of its unparalleled combination of quality and breadth; its high standards; its open, collaborative, and innovative culture; the opportunities provided by beautiful, vibrant rural and

urban campuses; and programs that extend throughout the state of New York and across the globe.

Retrieved June 26, 2012, from http://www.cornell.edu/about/mission/

University of Minnesota History and Mission excerpt

...In all of its activities, the University strives to sustain an open exchange of ideas in an environment that embodies the values of academic freedom, responsibility, integrity, and cooperation; that provides an atmosphere of mutual respect, free from racism, sexism, and other forms of prejudice and intolerance; that assists individuals, institutions, and communities in responding to a continuously changing world; that is conscious of and responsive to the needs of the many communities it is committed to serving; that creates and supports partnerships within the University, with other educational systems and institutions, and with communities to achieve common goals; and that inspires, sets high expectations for, and empowers individuals within its community.

Retrieved June 26. 2012 from http://www1.umn.edu/twincities/history-mission/index.html

University of San Francisco Mission

The core mission of the University is to promote learning in the Jesuit Catholic tradition. The University offers undergraduate, graduate and professional students the knowledge and skills needed to succeed as persons and professionals, and the values and sensitivity necessary to be men and women for others.

The University will distinguish itself as a diverse, socially responsible learning community of high quality scholarship and academic rigor sustained by a faith that does justice. The University will draw from the cultural, intellectual and economic resources of the San Francisco Bay Area and its location on the Pacific Rim to enrich and strengthen its educational programs.

Retrieved June 26, 2012 from http://www.usfca.edu/ about/values/

Any of these statements is a fine example of the values and expectations in American higher education. A well-intended college or university indeed strives to meet these self-defined standards. However, if a bully is in the midst, even this single individual can put a subordinate or the entire staff in a difficult position and distanced from that stated collaboration, creativity, and justice while being the target of aggression and incivility. If a bully is present, a target exerts a great deal of emotional labor to achieve these lofty cultural organizational goals, and the bully is an instrument that can take an institution away from its stated mission. Further, as many studies confirm, a bully acts as such because he or she is *allowed to be hostile*. Consequently, in the presence of a sustained bully, the organization is allowing this hostile figure to create a toxic work environment that deters the organization from the very mission and vision it has set for itself. Regardless of organizational levels, those toiling under the effects of a bully expend a great deal of emotional energy in an effort to remain focused on organizational tasks, and to do so with a smile.

Intersection of Bullying and Harassment: Bullrassment

As previously stated, bullying is pervasive, demeaning behavior that creates a toxic environment, while harassment is consistent, belittling, and escalating. Although harassment is the same type of behavior; by EEOC definitions, harassment statues only protect a protected status (race, gender, age, disability etc.). Therefore, a new term, *bullrassment,* which refers to bullying-harassment for people regardless of Title VII status, appropriately categorizes the issue.

American society is struggling with school bullying and its effects on young people. The media is chock full of stories about young people tormented by schoolyard bullies. As incivility and aggressive behavior follow people into adulthood, court cases and record numbers of formal complaints cite harassment as defined by Title VII, which shields people of protected classes from unequal treatment because of their race, gender, religion, color, or national origin. However, when the harassment/bullying occurs between two people of the same protected class, the target often doesn't have the same legal avenues for protection from discrimination or harassment. Status-free bullying—or bullrassment, status-free harassment by a bully—is currently legal (in 2012), although many states have introduced legislation against bully abuse. In 2010, the Workplace Bullying Survey reported that 13.7 million American adults are currently being bullied (Namie & Namie, 2009).

Development of Terms to Reflect Societal Demands

The development of a new term and coining a word to appropriately capture the breadth and severity of a situation is adapting the language to cultural and societal demands. The term "sexual harassment" was coined and used early in the 1970s and was used formally in a report to the chancellor at MIT to discuss gender relations on campus. Judicial precedence arose in *Williams v. Saxbe*, 413 F. Supp. 654, 657-61 (D.D.C. 1976*)*, when a lower court acknowledged and supported the notion that sexual harassment is an off shoot of sex discrimination, an illegal practice as defined by the 1964 Civil Rights Act. In 1986, the Supreme Court affirmed in *Meritor Savings Bank v. Vinson* that sexual harassment in the workplace is illegal, citing the EEOC regulations regarding sex discrimination as the foundation of its ruling.

As society considers the contemporary workplace, where the aggressive survive and withstand layoffs and budget cuts, the bullying abuse has been tolerated, even accepted and championed, in some corporate cultures. Nonetheless, currently there are no EEOC rules or advice relative to bullying. Bullying has become "bullrassment" in the workplace. Targets of bullying can formally complain under harassment and discrimination legislation if the target is from a Title VII-protected class. However when bullrassment occurs between two people of the same status, for example between two men, or between two colleagues over forty years of age, the charge that bullying is discrimination is disallowed. Nonetheless, the emotional damage to staff and the fiscal damage to the organization can be just as severe.

In 2001, Joe Doescher sued cardiologist Dr. Dan Raess for damages after he left his job due to emotional distress. Raess assaulted Doescher and charged him with a clenched fist. In 2008, a jury awarded $325,000 in what is considered the first US bullying trial. In 2005, two employees shared a $1.4 million settlement against CUNY. The two plaintiffs were humiliated, demoted, and subject to career threatening decisions.

A bully emerges regardless of gender, age, or sexual orientation. Bullying is a power play to achieve self-esteem by the humiliation of another student, co-worker, or subordinate. The bully, like the harasser, seeks out an empathetic personality who initially seems like an easy mark or target, someone whom the bully believes can be coerced. The bully, like a harasser, is subject to the same Title VII laws, but there are no specific anti-bullying laws on the books. Regardless of the technical legality of bullying, note that over 18% of disability claims stem from the emotional distress caused by a bully (Namie and Namie, 2009). Twenty-five percent of the people who are bullied leave the organization (Rayner, 2006).

Bullrassment, like sexual harassment, is the product of an unfortunate trend in workplace behavior. Even in the current absence of formal anti-bullying legislation, everyone deserves a healthy workplace. Beyond the plea for a civil workplace, managers and executives can save their organizations millions of dollars by facing bullrassment head on with zero tolerance policies.

Scope, Limitations, and Delimitations of this study

Ethical data collection research standards were critical for this social science research. The Collaborative Institutions Training Initiative (CITI) standards for human subjects were strictly applied during data collection. This informed consent process allowed for participants to contribute their perspectives anonymously without any personally identifiable data. They were able to withdraw from the study or make contact with the primary researcher at any time. The informed consent stated explicitly that there are no risks to the participant for contributing his or her perspectives.

This researcher receives annual training and certification of completion for the CITI, and standards for human subjects were strictly applied during the data collection in February and March

2012. During the data collection, it became clear that a number of participants would not complete the survey through their office computers. At first analysis, it appeared that over a third of the participants sent the link to a third party system to complete the data privately on a remote server. A few of the participants wrote or called to express appreciation for the research, and also expressed concern about whether their participation would be revealed. Many did not want to be discovered by their home institutions. While any researcher is bound by the CITI standards to protect the human subjects, the initial response of the participants confirms the continued need for confidentiality in dealing with human subjects.

The population for this study included 3200 participants from four-year colleges and universities from across the East Coast. This population was chosen to include large state institutions, private colleges and universities, Ivy League universities, and historically black colleges and universities. In turn, the limitations reflect that schools in the Central, Mountain, and Western time zones were not included in the data collection procedures; however, it is reasonable to assume that higher education at the four-year level is relatively consistent. Other limitations reflect the absence of the community college sector and proprietary education sector. Community college environments tend to rely heavily on unionized staff. The dynamic of workplace bullying with the influence and strength of a union was therefore outside the scope of this study. Further, proprietary education is often a hybrid model, with business and corporate expectations imposed on educational practice.

Therefore, proprietary education tends to be a faster paced and stress inducing educational environment. As stress is a major contributing factor to workplace bullying, a reasonable person might assume that proprietary education would also be a viable sector for research on workplace bullying; however, neither community colleges nor proprietary colleges were included in this study.

Chapter Two

Get the Bull Out of Work

B ullying is an extension of unchecked bad behavior that can emerge at any organizational level and influence people at work, play, and in relationships. Destructive bullying behavior demoralizes people regardless of the venue. Once thought of as simply a childhood rite of passage, bullying has become an international problem with studies since the 1990s examining this phenomenon in corporate and European structures.

Beyond the academic focus, bullying also is a common topic in popular culture and the nightly news, in film, fairy tales, and reports of incivility at work and school. The representation of bullying in private and professional arenas accentuates the extent of the problem. To that end, this chapter strives to reflect on not only previous academic findings, but also to consider the popular culture's representation of bullying which tends to minimize this problem at school and work.

"You know I'm bad...I'm really, really bad..."
—Michael Jackson, *Bad*, 1987

Popular culture is often a reflection of its own communities, echoing the preferences and interests of its participants. The reciprocal popular culture exchange of iconography, color, and energy emerge through the television, movies, and sporting events. When Michael Jackson and his "Bad" video were all the rage, grown men would wear those red or black asymmetric leather jackets with high-water pants, white socks, and a single glove. Over the years, whether it's Jennifer Aniston's signature hair, the impact of Michigan's Fab Five on athletic clothing, or even rap's impact on just about everything else, popular culture is an illustrative barometer often reflecting the temperament of the society.

Consequently, bullying and the issues facing the targets are an age-old story that also emerges through popular culture. Popular films such as *The Karate Kid*, *The Devil Wears Prada*, and even the Disney classic, *Cinderella*, focus on bullying and how the targets prevail, on their own, and escape unreasonable physical and psychological abuse.

Both iterations of *The Karate Kid* (1984 and 2010) tell of a young boy who relocates unexpectedly to another school. As the odd child out, Daniel (1984)/ Dre (2010) is teased, harassed, and even physically threatened. His escape is to defend himself through the sage wisdom and training of Mr. Miygi (1984)/ Mr. Han (2010). Regardless of the version, the message is clear: the weak and different are preyed upon and subjected to physical abuse. Though the martial arts tutor reminds the protégé that fighting should be about self-defense, the bottom line is those who adopt aggression prevail and are celebrated.

While reflecting on the domestic sphere, *Cinderella* illustrates how the marginalized character is overworked and devalued by a dominant culture. Cinderella finds herself struggling to please her stepmother and evil step-sisters. Their tactics, in addition to the cackling and insults, include unreasonable tasks and expectations. On several occasions, Cinderella is left toiling alone, without empathy or support. Unfortunately, as with the previous examples, art here imitates life.

The fantasy ensues as the fairy godmother whisks her away to the ball with a chariot and glass slippers where she is then validated by her prince charming. Unlike the real life targets of bullying, Cinderella truly is a fairy tale, since resolution relies on magic, not a messy lawsuit, job loss, or series of counseling appointments that bring her peace from the tyranny of bullies.

In a 2008 video op-ed piece, the *New York Times* references the character of Amanda Priestly in *The Devil Wears Prada*, the revered perpetrator of workplace bullying. This high-end fashion magazine executive is notorious for berating and demoralizing those around her through her subdued yet razor-sharp delivery of insults and demands. She decides to take a chance and hire the "smart fat girl;" enter Andy, a young woman writer looking for her break in the industry. The film continues with Andy being the constant target of incivility as she initially refuses to trade her plebeian, academic garb for a slick Parisian wardrobe that no one could possibly afford on her salary. The redeeming point of this scenario—despite the fact that Andy must acquiesce to Amanda's demands if she wants to find success at *Runway* magazine—is that Andy not only slays the dragon lady with her work performance to become the first assistant, she throws it all away to reclaim her own voice by the conclusion of the film.

The Andrea/Andy character, is a smart Northwestern graduate, pretty, and fat by no standards at a size six, yet her experience as portrayed in this highly stylized film is reportedly based on a true story. Similar to studies regarding bullying, this character endures criticism that has precious little to do with her work performance; nonetheless, her individualism initially makes her an oddity and fair game for bullying, similar to the real life experiences of workplace targets of bullying.

Consistent with the art-imitates-life concept, these dynamics are akin to the us-versus-them dynamic presented by Gordon Allport (1977). Human nature often seeks to ostracize the different, the odd, and the unexplained. Natural psychological reaction includes first avoidance, then insult, escalating to injury and violence. Allport claims that prejudice is based on this human nature; bullying as well aligns with Allport's hypothesis. Bullies often target those who are perceived as different or weak. Further, West (1994) addresses these conflicts through what he deems xenophobia, a fear of the different, foreign or unknown. His commentary fortifies the notion that in a dominating culture, those with power will use their power to act on their fear of the unfamiliar. Both ideologies point to fear and a presumed threat of the unknown as the root for aggression to contain that presumed threat. Consequently, the marginalized figure (whether Daniel/Dre, Cinderella, or Andy) are on the receiving end of escalating hostility. Until each character proves they are worthy or achieves validation through force or acquiescence, the bullying continues. Art imitates life.

In real life, the target of a bully doesn't have a fairy godmother to save the day. Instead, the target must assert some power or seek validation to eliminate bullying. Those who are in the less powerful position, organizationally or culturally, are more likely to be the target of a bully. When bullying occurs at work, any organization loses thousands of work hours when employees expend emotional labor to manage aggression instead of focusing on the organization's mission.

The Devil is in the Details

While few studies have addressed workplace bullying in American higher education, and none have addressed the manifestation of workplace bullying in American higher education administration, several studies in the last twenty years have examined workplace bullying in corporate structures and in European higher education. The similarities reveal a demoralized position for the target, which often toils with minimal support and then consequently transitions from the toxic position to regain a sense of self.

Namie and Namie have contributed a salient work in *The Bully at Work*, which reports on their findings from a 2007 partnership with Zogby International. They define workplace bullying as a "silent epidemic," where 37% of American workers claim they have been bullied at work. Additional findings state that 49% of workers are affected by workplace bullying—24% have been bullied at some time, 12% have witnessed bullying, and 13% are presently enduring bullying.

The same study reveals that women are disproportionately targets of workplace bullying, as women are the target 71% of the time when women are the bullies and 46% of the time when men are the bullies. To find relief from bullying, the target quits 40% of the time and is fired 24% of the time. Moreover, 44% of the time the organization did nothing to provide relief for the targets. In 18% of the cases, the situation became worse for the target once bullying was reported (Namie and Namie, 2009, p. 4-11).

European studies (Einarsen, Hoek, Zapf, & Cooper, 2003) document that 65% of those who took the Negative Acts Survey had some kind of exposure to workplace bullying. High exposure to incivility was claimed by 8% of respondents. A study of Norwegian shipyard workers revealed that 88% of respondents had experienced workplace bullying. The duration of bullying often occurs at least over six months, yet the mean is approximately 18 months, while some data from Ireland reveal bullying lasting over three years (pp. 11-15). As with other studies, bullying originated with an imbalance of power (p. 15) where the target lacks the power to respond or defend.

A study from the United Kingdom (Thomas, 2010) reports that 34% of respondents in higher education had been bullied in the previous six months, compared to 11% of respondents in all occupations. Bullying was not reported by 69%; however, of those who did report the bullying, their respective organizations responded poorly to the reports of workplace incivility. Thomas reports that bullying included "unreasonable or impossible deadlines, being given an unmanageable workload, and being subject to excessive monitoring of work" (para 6).

Further, another survey of 5000 British employees reveals that over one million work days had been lost to workplace bullying because one in ten workers had stress stemming from workplace bullying (Keelan, 2000). A Canadian study revealed that 78% of respondents felt incivility on the job "had worsened in the previous ten years" (Pearson, 1999).

Those who suffer as the targets of workplace bullying also suffer health issues. Hypertension, weight gain, sleep issues, and elevated stress are among results for the target of workplace bullying. Post-traumatic stress and hypertension also can occur for those who suffer under a workplace bully. Rayner (1998) found that 75.6% of employees who reported being bullied experience negative health effects. Further, 73% of those who witnessed bullying also endured health problems. Many lost their confidence and self-esteem. Sleep problems developed along with depression, lack of concentration, stomach problem, moodiness, anxiety, and higher susceptibility to colds (Thomas, 2005, p. 282).

The aforementioned provides insight to the breadth of the bullying problem internationally and in the United States. Whether in factual or fictional accounts, power corrupts when those who exercise aggression have minimal accountability for their actions. Therefore, an organizational and leadership model that incorporates checks and balances at all levels of an organization can develop preventative measures to minimize workplace aggression and bullying.

Chapter Three

Bullying in American Higher Education Administration

D uring February 2012, over 3200 participants were asked to complete the Hollis Workplace Bullying in the Academy Survey (WBAS). The population comprised staff of four-year colleges and universities. While these findings are generalizable to the community college and proprietary sectors in higher education, these latter two types of systems were outside the scope of the study. As no other survey existed to specifically examine workplace bullying in higher education administration, the researcher created a new instrument which was beta-tested for reliability by seven professionals in higher education administration before the official launch of the study. The researcher used Survey Monkey to host the thirty-five question instrument and collect incoming data. Each of 175 colleges or universities that comprised the population received 18 invitations to staff to participate in the study. Two participants were selected from each of the following: athletics, student affairs, information technology (IT), human resources, executive level, admissions/financial aid, academic faculty (science), academic faculty (arts), and external affairs/development.

Through a five week data collection period via email, 14% of the population (448) was unreachable as email invitations bounced back due to protections on university and college servers. Another 5% of the population opted out of the study (161). Of the remaining 2,592 in the sample, 15.5% (n= 401) completed the informed consent process and subsequent survey.

After the data was analyzed, it was determined that close to 62% of respondents in the Hollis WBAS study confirmed that they had been bullied or witnessed bullying in their higher education positions in the last 18 months. In contrast, the 62% of those reporting workplace bullying in higher education is significantly higher than the 37% of those reporting corporate workplace bullying in the Namie and Namie (2009) study. In short, higher education administration employees face workplace bullying 58% more often than corporate employees. Further, 53% of the higher education respondents in the Hollis WBAS study are actively trying to leave their positions, or report that they would leave if other positions were available. Also, over half of the respondents sent the link to the survey to a remote location to avoid responding at work. A few confirmed in their open-ended questions that, while they wanted to participate in the survey, they were afraid that the organization or supervisor would track their responses.

By the numbers—Demographics

Regarding demographics, 67% of the participants were white, 20% were black, 3% were Asian, 5% were Hispanic and 5% claimed a multi-race affiliation. Women were 72% of the respondents.

Demographics

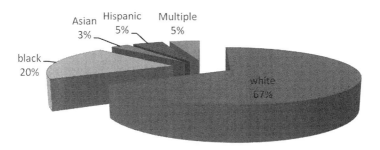

Gender

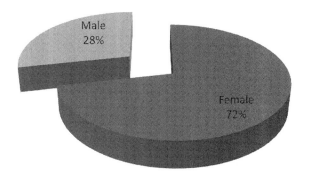

Ninety-one percent of respondents were heterosexual, while 9% were from the lesbian, bisexual/gay/ transgender (LBGT) community. In regard to age, 30%, the highest percentage of respondents, were 50–60 years of age; 25% of respondents were 40–49 years of age. Fourteen percent were over 60 and 13% were 35–40 years of age.

Sexual Orientation

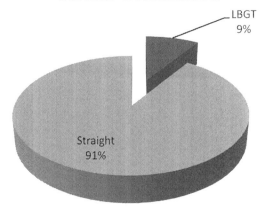

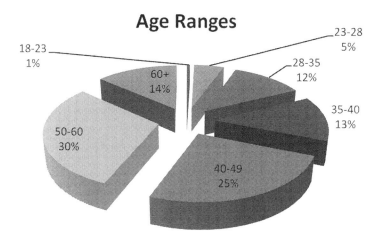

Salary Ranges

While all salary ranges were surveyed, the highest concentrations of salary ranges were 16% earning $40–45,000 per year, 15% of respondents earning $65,000–75,000 per year, and 14% making $55–65,000 per year. After excluding the fifteen salaries over $150,000, the mean salary across 381 respondents is 67,636. They would on average earn a monthly rate of $5636 (assuming a 40 hours week) or $135.22 an hour. This mean annual salary is lower than the $87,000 reported by the Bureau of Labor Statistics for post-secondary administrators.

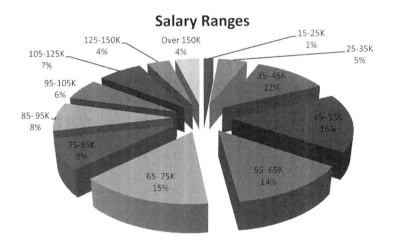

Salary Ranges

Which groups are bullied?

The general population, with n= 401, reported that 62% of respondents had been bullied or witnessed bullying in higher education administration in the last 18 months. Forty-five percent of the general population reported that they had been the target of or witnessed vicarious bullying (when a bully empowers a subordinate to do the bullying) in the last 18 months. Proportionately, African Americans, women, and members of the LBGT community experience proportionally higher levels of bullying. For African Americans, with n= 84, 80% of African American respondents had been bullied or witnessed bullying in higher education in the last 18 months. Fifty-five percent of the African American population reported that they had been the target of, or witnessed vicarious bullying in the last 18 months. With n= 281,

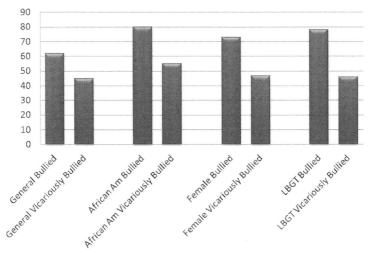

73% of women respondents had been bullied or witnessed bullying in higher education in the last 18 months. Of the women, 47% reported that they had been the target of or had witnessed vicarious bullying in the last 18 months. For the LBGT community, with n= 31, 78% of the respondents reported they had been bullied or witnessed bullying in higher education in the last 18 months. The LBGT community population reported that 46% had been the target of or had witnessed vicarious bullying in the last 18 months.

Men represented 28% of the respondents (n=111). Over 75% of the male respondents were over forty years of age. Forty-six percent of male respondents had earned a doctorate. Forty-two percent of men reported that they had experienced or witnessed bullying in the last 18 months. While 42% is below the average for this study, the 42% rate of bullying that men reported in this study is still above the 37% national rate reported by Namie and Namie (2009).

Educational Level and Job Titles

The highest concentration of the respondents hold masters degrees (45%) and hold doctoral degrees (36%).

While all levels of the organization received invitations to participate, no presidents responded. The highest percentage (24%) of respondents came from the director level and 17% of respondents were from the assistant director level.

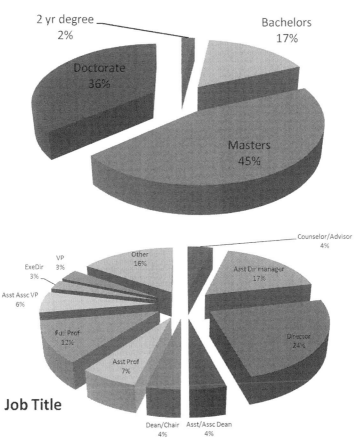

Target of Bullying in Higher Education

As n=401, 176 participants (44%) claimed that they had not witnessed or experienced bullying in the last 18 months. Thirty percent (122) stated that they had experienced bullying in the last 18 months, and 36% stated that they witnessed bullying in the last 18 months. This question allowed for multiple answers. Sixteen of the respondents had both witnessed and experienced bullying. Once the 16 duplicates respondents and removed from the calculation, 249 participants, or 62% of 401 respondents stated that they had witnessed or experience bullying in higher education in the last 18 months.

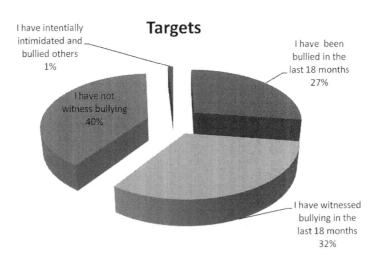

Vicarious Bullying

For the purpose of this study, the researcher introduced the term "vicarious" bullying to describe leaders and managers who send or authorize subordinates or junior staff members to wield their executive power. A leader can use this tactic to continue intimidation in his or her absence, or use it in an attempt to preserve a façade of kindness while using subversive tactics to control staff. Fifty-eight percent stated that they had not witnessed or experienced vicarious bullying. Twenty-five percent have witnessed vicarious bullying while 16% have been the target of vicarious bullying. One percent admitted to using vicarious bullying as an intimidation tactic.

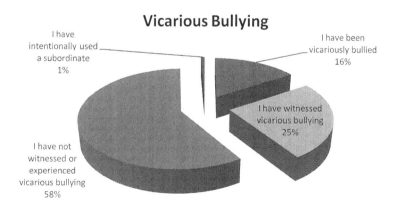

Vicarious Bullying

- I have intentionally used a subordinate 1%
- I have been vicariously bullied 16%
- I have witnessed vicarious bullying 25%
- I have not witnessed or experienced vicarious bullying 58%

Toxic Work Environment

When asked if a toxic work environment affected service or performance at work, respondents indicated that morale, internal service to staff, and compliance with policy and regulations were definitely affected.

Toxic Definitely affected:

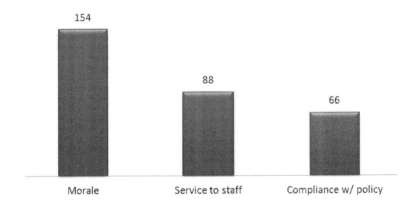

Toxic Work Environment Didn't Affect

Respondents also indicated that enrollment, academic integrity, and customer service externally were definitely not affected.

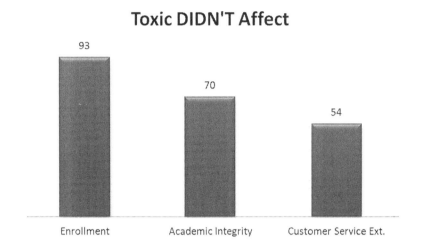

Toxic DIDN'T Affect

Least Likely to Have Bullying

When asked which areas of a university were least likely to endure a bully with choices of athletics, academics–arts, academics–science, admissions/financial aid, executives, development/external affairs, human resources, IT department, and student affairs, respondents stated that human resources, student affairs, and the IT department were the least likely places that endured a bully.

Least likely to endure bullying

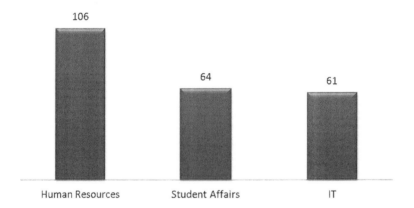

Most Likely to Have Bullying

When asked which areas of a university where most likely to endure a bully with choices of athletics, academics-arts, academics- science, admissions/financial aid, executives, development/external affairs, human resources, IT department, and student affairs, respondents stated that the executive level, academics-arts, athletics, and academic-science were the most likely places that endured a bully.

Most likely to endure bullying

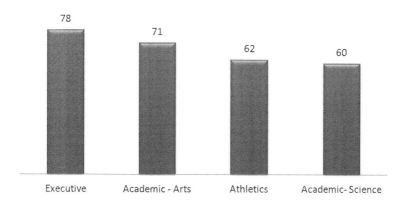

Educational level of target

Relative to the educational level of the target, consistent with other information on workplace bullying, the target tends to hold the least amount of power. Those with a master's degree are the target 25% of the time. Those with only a bachelor's degree are the target 20% of the time, while those with doctorates are targets 15% of the time. As few positions in this study at four-year higher education institutions allow for only a high school degree or two-year degrees, only 8% of participants and 5% of participants from those groups respectively were the target of workplace bullying.

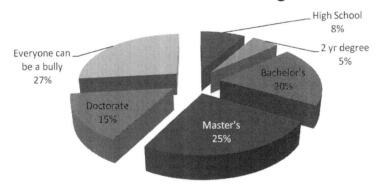

Educational Level of Target

While 32.1% of respondents in the following question stated that they had not witnessed bullying, similar to the findings on educational level, and other information on workplace bullying, the target tends to hold the least amount of power. Compared to other job titles, participants at the entry level were bullied 28.8% of the time and assistant directors were the target of bullying 19.2% of the time.

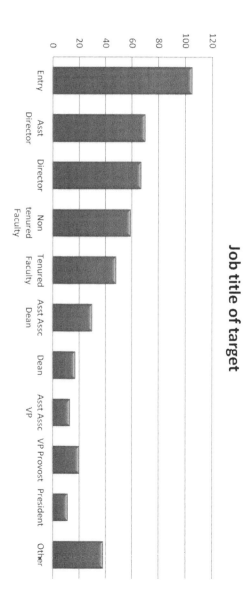

Where Bullying Occurs

Twenty-seven percent of the respondents stated that they were bullied in a one-on-one meeting while 25% stated that they were bullied in front of staff. Workplace bullying also occurs in a local staff meeting (14%), through cyberspace (14%), at a division-wide staff meeting (9%) and in front of students (8%) of the time.

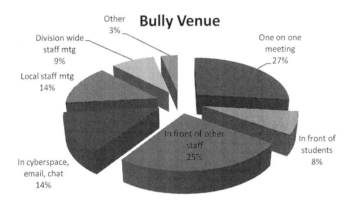

Other open ended responses which address where bullying occurs include:

- In the hallway on the way to meetings
- It has been more covert, but other staff and students have been engaged in the process
- By telephone
- Behind someone's back—in secret—but decision impactful
- Ad-hoc meeting

How targets are bullied

Fifty-three percent of respondents reported that being overlooked and ignored were common tactics for the bully. Close to 53% also reported that yelling and insults were common tactics of the bully. Harshly written harassment memos and notes were reported by 47% of the respondents and being the subject of group gossip was cited 43% of the time. Respondents were asked to "check all that apply" in regard to the question, "How are targets bullied?" The responses overlapped with the sum of the percentages reporting over 100%.

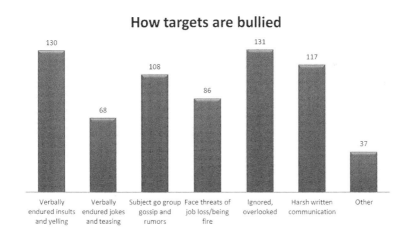

How targets are bullied

Other open-ended responses regarding how targets are bullied include:

- Teamed up with subordinate to trap me
- Being told one thing in a face-to-face meeting where a

mutual understanding was achieved... then later in evening via email...explained the exact opposite and threatened with discipline

- Increasing continuously the work load without regard to employee dumping
- During appraisal/evaluations telling me that I am "not entitled" to concerns in comments section
- Manipulated with vague threats; positioned concerns as illegitimate; lectured about tacit protocol and inappropriateness of agreement; silenced through the abandonment of financial support; controlled through lack of budget line; refusal to find organizational home for the program
- Libel, false accusations of inappropriate behavior, and conflict of interest, false accusation of criminal activity

Organizational Bullying

In regard to organizational tactics which keep targets off balance, 18% stated their goals were changed without notice (changed deadlines or objectives), 16% reported that they were assigned unreasonable tasks, and another 16% were subject to unreasonable accountability (minute-by-minute updates). Thirteen percent reported that they were excluded from social gatherings and another 13% reported their responsibilities (budget, reporting structure) were changed abruptly without notice.

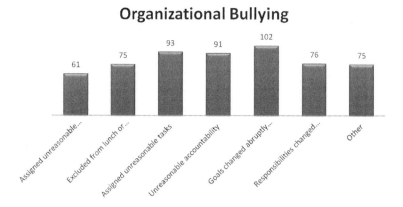

Organizational Bullying

Other open ended responses regarding organizational bullying include:

- Given tasks without guidance and set up for failure
- Not given same opportunities or situations as others less travel, smaller budget, requiring more documentation and reports
- Told work was unimportant and could be replaced by a "monkey"
- Responsibilities unclear and requests for explanations ignored
- Not provided with policy driven documentation such as evaluations. This sets up a system where the absence of documentation can be used against the target.

Duration of Bullying

Twenty-seven percent of respondents stated that bullying occurs more than three calendar years, 26% stated that bullying occurred for two to three calendar years. In open-ended questions, many commented that bullying occurred much longer than the three-year window offered in the survey.

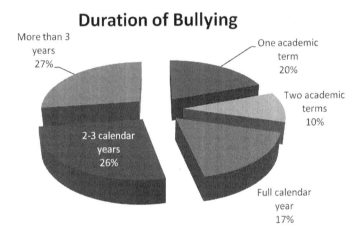

Duration of Bullying

Target Reaction

Twenty-six percent of the targets reported that they isolated themselves in the face of a bully. Nineteen percent reported the bullying to the supervisor; 16% quit; 15% reported the problem to human resources; and 14% took more sick time.

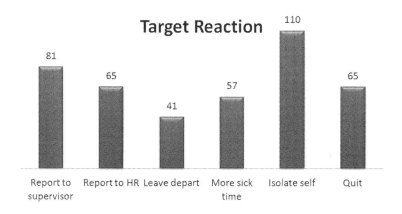

Other open ended responses regarding how targets respond to bullying include:

- Resented ineffectiveness of HR
- Committed suicide (knew colleague who went to such lengths)
- Cry
- File complaint of harassment
- One person tried to stand strong, but the stress of situation caused health problems
- Medication and therapy

Target Strategies

Thirty-three percent of respondents stated that the target found no relief from workplace bullying in higher education. Fifteen percent of respondents stated that targets isolated themselves from the group; 10% of respondents stated that bullying was reported to the supervisor; 10% of respondents stated that the target left the department.

Target strategies for relief

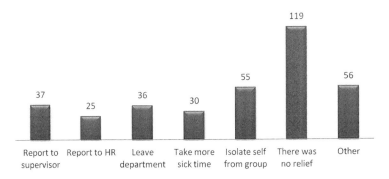

Other open ended responses in regard to target strategies include:

- Suicide
- Prayer
- Hope new dean will stop problem
- Pretend it's not so bad
- Access employee assistance programs

Time Spent Avoiding

Twenty-three percent of respondents reported that an hour each week was spent avoiding the bully. Twenty-two percent reported that a full week was spent avoiding the bully. Sixteen percent reported that 2 hours weekly was spent avoiding the bully. When the strata of responses are calculated into a mean answer, 3.9 hours are spent weekly trying to avoid the bully.

Weekly time spent avoiding bully

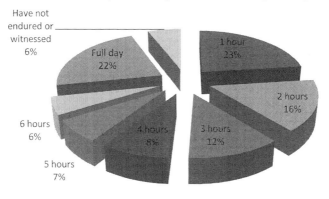

Target Left or Separated from Department

Over half of the respondents reported that at least one person left the department as a result of bullying. Thirteen percent of respondents reported that two people left; and 11% reported that three had left. Eight percent of respondents stated that more than six people had left the department in the last 18 months to avoid the toxic work environment created by a workplace bully.

Target left or separated from department

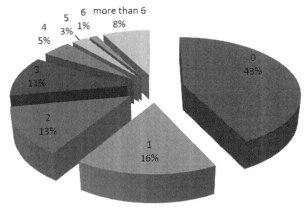

Who is the Bully?

Twenty-two percent of respondents stated that the director is likely to be the bully. Fourteen percent reported that tenured faculty tend to be the bully. Twelve percent reported that the dean is the bully. Eleven percent reported that the assistant vice president or assistant vice provost was the bully. Note the majority of the respondents to this study are from middle management.

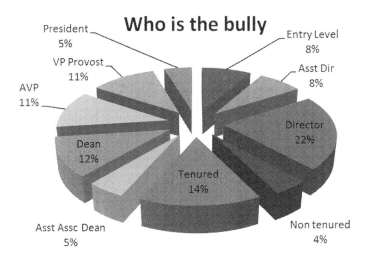

Organization Response to a Bully

Twenty-eight percent of respondents stated that the organization did nothing to deal with the bully. Nineteen percent reported that the organization supported the bully. Nineteen percent of respondents said the bully was transferred to another department. Eighteen percent said the bully was coached. Seven percent said that the target was transferred. Five percent said that the target was fired; and 4% said the bully was fired.

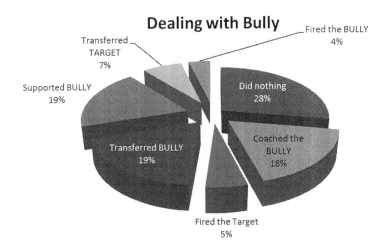

Bullying and departure

Twenty-two percent report that they thought about leaving, but there are few positions to apply to in the current job market. Seventeen percent report that the bullying problem is not bad enough for them to leave their job. Fifteen percent report that they have tried to leave because of a bully, but the job market keeps them in their current position.

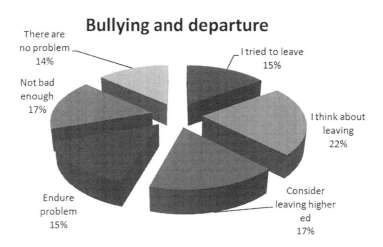

Open Ended Responses and Comments

Participants were asked to offer additional remarks about workplace bullying. One hundred nineteen (119) additional comments were collected. The researcher is choosing twenty-eight (28) of the remarks which are representative of the pool. In addition to the general remarks, comments tend to align around three themes, EEO concerns, faculty concerns, and executive leadership.

Theme #1 General remarks on workplace bullying in higher education:

- [This is] a chronic, pervasive problem that undermines the effectiveness and integrity of higher education.

- Sometimes it feels like you are being discriminated against because you offer an element of professionalism and expertise in areas. Jealousy is part of the problem. Not wanting to see any one excel beyond their current status. It could be avoidable. It is extremely frustrating. Causes severe anxiety. I have taken it for many years. Much too long.

- I have never experienced it until this year and have been fortunate to have found another position in which I do not directly report to the bully but still have her in my purview as she works in my department. Working under her for about 8 months was so devastating, I had to seek professional counseling and tried to report her but did not trust the system to actually do anything about it but make me look like a tattler. It is absolutely devastating to be in the midst of a very successful professional career and come across a bully. You don't expect it, you can't believe it and you are not prepared to deal with it and most organizations have nothing in place to help you.

> It is devastating to be in the midst of a very successful career and come across a bully.

- I left my previous institution in part because they permitted a coach in the athletic department to bully everyone and anyone. It created an awful work environment yet everyone from HR to the president of the university felt it didn't reach harassment status so there was nothing to be done about it. This was allowed to continue until the man finally retired.

Theme #2 Remarks regarding executive leadership and bullying in higher education:

- When there was a bullying incident at the workplace several years ago, it was reported to the Ombudsman. That person who is also the head of HR ran to the president's office. The Provost then called the victim into his office and threatened the female victim with her job. They then refused to hand over the diaries which documented the constant abuse. We have workshops, presentations, and an Ombudsman. It is all a load of crap.
- The political gamesmanship should not be allowed to happen.

Faculty are protected and so should all staff so that executives cannot make them feel lesser than, or bully them.

- It comes from the top, the president and his/her cabinet (the heads of operations who report directly to him/her).

- High level administrators must express a zero tolerance stance on bullying.

- Deans are likely to be perpetrators or conspirators in bullying without intervention from anyone in the university.

- Department chairs must be vigilant. This means spotting bullying behavior. Once identified, attempts should be made to mentor both the bully and the target to change behavior in a positive way for both parties.

- I think bullying trickles down from the top starting with executives working its way down to building and maintenance staff. If the administration threatens job loss, write-ups and reduced pay, then the intermediate level chair and supervisor will do the same.

> I think bullying trickles down from the top.

- I think the worst kind of bullying that I have witnessed occurred by a university president who yelled and screamed at a room full of faculty, staff, and administrators. This president threw papers down on the floor, showed aggressive body language, and actually yelled at the group. This kind of behavior is unbecoming of any university president, and is inexcusable. This behavior was witnessed by the provost and other administrators and none of them stopped it nor did they do anything to resolve the situation. The worst bullying occurs at the executive level and this destroys morale. Since this event, I am absolutely ashamed of and have lost respect for our upper level administrators who show no admission of wrong doing. [This] tells us that administrators in upper administrations are not fit for effective leadership. Most people who value themselves as leaders would have taken action to address their own inappropriate behavior.

- It seems to me that the president of the institution has a great deal of power. He, himself, is a bully and those individuals whom he favors are also bullies.

- I experienced a bully boss who reported to the president. He [the president] refused to address the problem despite written requests and visits from HR. I quit last year to get away from the toxic environment. HR acknowledged the problem and appealed to the president, but the president supports the bully.

- I think upper level leadership, deans, and department heads need training on dealing with issues of bullying. Education about a diverse campus in terms of students and faculty needs research

> I think upper leadership needs training on dealing with bullying.

agendas, research methodologies, and campus wide accountability created and implemented relative to bullying.

- I was victimized by a department chair and staff at a previous institution (a major AAU university). Where I have witnessed and experienced bullying, the approach of upper administrators is usually misguided and ineffectual. This is almost a generic problem and a very serious issue that hurts esprit de corps; costs efficiency, and can create legal problems if not caught early.

Theme #3 Remarks regarding Human Resources and EEO

- I have been surprised by men in lower-level staff (IT, Security) positions, bullying women employees, including support staff and faculty.
- HR is of no help whatsoever when the bully has brought in a million dollars for the institution and the bully is the president's buddy. Three individuals were harassed by this individual before she was finally removed as department chair.
- Bullying is a significant problem that is usually glossed over as 'personality conflict' or just having a tough boss or leader. I have held four jobs in fundraising in higher education; at three of the organizations, the toxic atmosphere was beyond oppressive and people were afraid to say anything. HR offices have

> **HR offices have usually protected bullies because they were senior staff.**

usually protected bullies because they were senior staff and the person being bullied was let go or left in frustration. I know a lot of people who have felt very let down by HR office and it would be helpful to have HR offer greater assistance and support. It gives you the confidence to not suffer in silence.

- I am a black female in science. In my first academic position, I was one of three black faculty members in the entire institution. My colleagues referred to me and the black female lab manager as the "affirmative action hires." One fellow non-tenured faculty member told me "nigger is gone by sun down." I reported it to the supervisor, the dean, and the vice-president. They promoted him and fired me. The lab supervisor quit mid-semester and I am enrolled in school to get out of academia all together. There is an EEOC case pending.

- This is a real problem in higher education—we are not immune. HR and legal counsel "get it" but don't want to address it with a policy; they suggest our non-discrimination policy is strong—but bullies are equal opportunity discriminators. I left my university once because of a bully. She has been promoted at least twice.

> I left my university once, because of a bully. She had been promoted twice.

- I think bullying is overlooked and Human Resources work for the institution and not the employee. I think therefore that HR is hoping that it will go away!

Theme #4 Remarks regarding faculty and bullying

- A stressful and competitive atmosphere encouraged bullying between faculty members. At a student level, years ago, I had to protect students who were bullied because of sexual orientation or gender issues.

- As a faculty member with tenure, I have talked about my problem of being bullied with an administrator at another institution. She remarked that by the time the reports of bullying get to her, it is a blood bath and she can't tell who the bully is.

- Tenured faculty and administrators with tenured faculty appointments are untouchables and thus they continuously get away with bullying because it isn't looked at as a termination worthy issue. Of course, when something drastic happens, i.e. a disgruntled employee lashes out after years of torment; the pendulum will swing towards zero tolerance. The norm is bullies running unchecked devouring the meek and weak in an organizational structure. The bullies pick on those that they believe they can bully but won't stand up against someone on equal footing. It is sad to watch.

> No one should be immune from repercussions.

- No one should be immune from repercussions. Faculty is often given carte blanche. I guess that's academic freedom...

- What I have experienced is the habit of an assistant dean distributing a list of faculty members who have failed to meet deadlines in submitting grades, to all faculty members and department chairs, so that dozens of people see who the "delinquents" are.

- It's been so destructive and depressing... in two of my jobs... in both cases from (faculty) chairpersons and faculty and in one case from the union. . .

- Untenured faculty is very susceptible to being bullied by their tenured colleagues; the whole system is set up to support that. Lots of senior colleagues have a hazing mentality— I suffered as an untenured faculty member so you should suffer too.

Elements of a Healthy Workplace in Higher Education

When asked if they had experienced a healthy workplace in higher education, participants were permitted to check all elements that apply. Respect from colleagues (n= 310), positive attitude of the boss (n=304), respect from administration (n=302), and the positive attitude of colleagues (n= 293) were the most important factors in creating a healthy workplace. Clear policies were named by 157 participants, training was named by 130 participants, and visible human resources department was named by only 81 participants.

ELEMENTS OF HEALTHY WORKPLACE

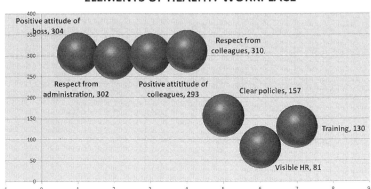

Below are several open-ended responses on what creates a healthy work environment in higher education. Six respondents took the time to report they had never experienced a healthy workplace during their career in higher education.

1. Consistent messages, no favoritism

2. When a healthy workplace environment was experienced, positive empowering comments and rewards were offered.

3. Trust, humility, and openness to try new things and especially the power to forgive when trust needs to be earned again

4. Self-respect, committees, councils, and policies that promote diversity

5. Leadership with enough ego strength to care about the mission and collaborative work beyond their personal power or advancement

6. Policies and training have no effect on disrespectful or abusive

behavior. The only thing that works is holding people (especially high ranking people) strictly accountable for this behavior—and providing colleagues and subordinates with resources to go for help when they are treated poorly and support for administrators in managing the problematic behavior.

7. Top down control with strong leadership
8. A no tolerance attitude toward bullying, including training sessions. Describe the phenomenon and how to deal with it.
9. Strong leadership from the top down
10. President's zero-tolerance policy
11. Accountability and transparency, genuine adherence to academic due process, fair application of disciplinary actions, a work culture that opposes bullying, a work culture that prevents bullying and takes effective action when bullying occurs

Cost of Bullying in Higher Education

There were 381 participants who answered the question about salary. Twenty respondents skipped the salary question. Of those 381 who did respond, 15 made over $150,000. As a salary range can't be determined for those 15, they were removed from the discussion on cost and salary. The remaining 366 have a mean salary of $67,636 or $5,636 per month resulting in an hourly rate of $35.22. While these numbers over represent salary for entry level and assistant director levels, the median salary establishes a working data point to consider the cost of workplace bullying. Please note this number is $20,000 less than the stated $87,000 salary reported by the Bureau of Labor Statistics for post-secondary administrators for 2012.

As stated earlier, 23% of respondents reported they spent an hour each week avoiding the bully. Twenty-two percent reported that a full day a week (8 hours) was spent avoiding the bully. When all responses were considered, the mean time was 3.9 hours spent weekly to deal with a workplace bully.

3.9 hours x 35. 22/hr. = 137.39 a week

137.39 x 50 weeks* = $6869.50 lost per person annually

*50 weeks was used to account for two weeks of professional holidays

Recall that 62% of respondents stated that they were the target of workplace bullying or witnessed workplace bullying in the last 18 months. Consider the following numbers which are loosely related to staffing respective colleges and universities. Note again $6869.50 is lost per person annually.

Annual Loss

	Medium Private	*Large State*	*Small Liberal Arts*
	1100 Staff	22000 staff	1900 Staff
X 62%	682 staff bullied	13640 staff bullied	1178 staff bullied
	682 x 6869.5	13640 x 6869.5	1178 x 6869.5
	$4,684,999	*$93,699,980*	*$8,092,271*

If 62% of higher education staff is affected by bullying, and as a result, when this staff disengages for 3.9 hours each week, then for example, a small liberal arts college with 1900 people on staff potentially is losing over $8 million by allowing workplace bullying. A large state university with 22000 on staff is potentially loosing over $93.5 million. A medium private school with 1100 on staff is potentially losing over $4.5 million annually because staff disengaged from work to strategize or worry about the tactics of a bully.

The replacement cost of turnover is also enormous. Background checks, advertisements, lost productivity, the cost of a search, rehiring, and retraining procedures can quickly cost 150% of the salary. For example, if an employee with the salary of $67,000 leaves the organization (the median salary of the participants in this study) the organization will spend $100,500 to replace that person (Bliss 2012; Jurnak, 2010).

The quantitative findings report that 16% of the targets leave the institution. The aforementioned information reveals that an institution loses150% of a salary when an employee leaves. The mean salary of the population is $67,000; therefore, below are the levels of loss due to turnover. Each position that is in turnover costs $100,500.

Annual Turnover Loss

	Medium Private	***Large State***	***Small Liberal Arts***
	1100 Staff	22000 staff	1900 Staff
X 16%	176 staff turnover	3520 staff turnover	304 staff turnover
	100,500 x 176	100,500 x 3520	100,500 x 304
	$17,688,000	$353,760,000	$30,552,000

If 16% of the higher education staff leaves a position because of bullying, then for example, a small liberal arts college with 1900 people on staff potentially is losing over $30 million dollars in turnover costs by allowing workplace bullying. A large state university with 22,000 on staff is potentially losing over $353 million in turnover costs. A medium private school with 1100 on staff is potentially losing over $17 million annually because of turnover cost related to bullying.

Chapter Four

Qualitative Findings on Workplace Bullying in Higher Education

In addition to the quantitative data collection, several qualitative interviews were conducted with higher education professionals. Their titles from various state, private, public, and historically black institutions are as follows: associate provost, assistant director, academic advising, regional director, director of financial aid, associate director of admissions, vice president of development, associate athletic director, and human resources trainer. To protect their anonymity only "participant" designations and themes were revealed in support of the quantitative findings. By using descriptive statistics and themes emerging from qualitative inquiry, the researcher develops theories about why workplace bullying is occurring in higher education specifically. Further, the emerging themes from both quantitative and qualitative findings will develop a model which will offer solutions to leadership in managing the ill effects of workplace bullying. Future studies may build on these findings to isolate an independent variable for in-depth statistical analysis. Presented below are the five themes and the most robust comments from participants supporting these themes. An interesting note: most of the quantitative participants represent middle management and offered quantitative remarks and open-ended statements from that middle organizational status. Of the qualitative interviews, one-third of the participants were cabinet level positions.

Architect of The Academy

Nine audio-taped interviews of 60–75 minutes in duration comprise the qualitative portion of this study. All participants agreed to the informed consent process and understood that only their titles, not institutions or names, would be used to report these findings. The qualitative interviews yielded five salient themes in regard to workplace bullying in higher education administration.

The themes are:

1. Leadership and organizational culture
2. Role of human resources/EEO office
3. Cost (lost through turnover and disengaged staff)
4. Coping strategies for individuals
5. Effect on services and functions

Closer analysis confirmed that executive leadership is truly the architect of the academy. The leader sets the tone for policy, the application of policy, and empowers the human resources department to advocate for a healthy workplace, regardless of the organizational level of the complainant. In short, the findings supported the idea that a leader who is truly committed to a healthy workplace and directly implements strategies to maintain that healthy workplace endures less cost from disengagement, less turnover, fewer lawsuits, and a more inspired and productive staff.

Theme #1: Leadership Drives Organizational Culture

All nine participants pointed to leadership and its effect on organizational culture as the main reason workplace bullying occurred in higher education administration. Leadership has the purview to set policy, empower staff, and create a culture that would either allow for aggression and incivility, or stop aggression and incivility. In many cases, as confirmed in the quantitative findings, the bully often was the boss or the leader, leaving subordinates at best disengaged, or at worst relinquishing their positions to find relief. Two participants of the nine in the interview pool reflected on healthy work environments. In each case, executive level leaders were particularly active in creating a healthy workplace, implementing policy, modeling civil behavior, and holding people accountable for aggressive behavior.

Participant #2 discussed the organizational culture in depth. Her three years at her large public institution were fraught with turnover, aggressive behavior from staff, and little support from executive ranks or human resources." I spend at least ten hours a week dealing with nasty people..." She spent an hour every morning fielding nasty and aggressive emails; she spent another thirty minutes daily taking abuse from her unionized secretarial pool,

> I feel like a
> DISPOSABLE
> employee...

and concluded the day dealing with more nasty remarks via phone or email. When asked about support from her boss, she commented that there had been three directors and two deans in three years. She remarked this was the result of an aggressive faculty union which ran roughshod over anyone without union protection. Over her three years on the job, faculty had threatened her job through several erroneous grievances designed to monopolize her time.

When asked about support from the vice president, she remarked there was no such support; this participant felt that she was only in place to protect executives or be the front line. She had been actively looking for a new job for over a year, but determined to go *to* a job instead of running *from* her current position. She was tired of walking on egg shells just to do her job, without having to endure aggressive and bullying behavior from unionized faculty.

Participant #1 reflected on the years working with an executive. While this person had not been the target of the bully, this person had watched as three administrative assistants were forced out of a position by an aggressive bully. When asked how the organization dealt with the problem, the response was "It is an open secret. . . . we just scramble to cover it up." In this case, the bully

> **It's an 'Open Secret'**

was the leader who set the tone for acceptable aggression on the job. "No one said any thing...we just stayed out of his way." Since he was the leader, he was not held accountable for his actions; he just kept getting new administrative assistants. The situation became so bad for one assistant, participant #1 ended up in a position to console the target. "I ran into her when she found out that her transfer out of the office had been delayed four months... she fell apart...just cried. What could I do? I held her in my arms while she just cried inconsolably when she realized her escape had been delayed..." Since this time, participant #1 has witnessed this target transfer away from the department. However, it appears the bully boss was never held accountable, and he has a new assistant.

In concluding remarks, participant #1 reflected on bullying behavior in higher education. This participant has served as faculty, in middle

> It is THAT ugly here.

management, and in executive leadership. In short, the comments reflected, "when there is no accountability, these things go on.... It is *that* ugly here.

Participant #3 had over 30 years in academic and athletic administration. In the current position, participant #3 had repeatedly reported problems with a department head to the vice president's and provost's offices. Despite the fact that there were ten departments heads in this area over the previous years, no one took notice of the problems... until two EEOC complaints for this area came to campus. Leadership turned a blind eye until it was too late. Everyone was hiring everyone else's friends.

Participant #9 offered an inverse experience from her unviersity. Her school had a well documented anti-bullying policy and civility policy. Not that the school didn't have bullying issues, but there was a structure from which to deal with these problems. Civility was part of the organizational culture and formal evaluation process. When asked what started this initiative, she clearly stated, "The president has made this a priority for years. He set the tone; he wanted the

> The president has made civility a priority for years.

policies; he modeled the behavior." The president led the way for civility in a very unionized campus and made it clear that good behavior was a way of campus life, not an exception.

Participant #8 had faced bullying at a previous institution. The experience left this participant in tears when retelling the story of belittling remarks, defamation, and harassment. Even after this person had left the previous institution, the bullying followed this person to the next institution in the form of defamation via email, memos, and blogs. Other targets from the previous institution had called participant #8 to ask about strategies for how to deal with this executive leader bully. Fearful of future retaliation, participant #8 didn't answer the calls. In regard to this workplace bullying study in the academy, participant #8 was particularly careful and commented about his/her fear in answering the survey and not wanting to be discovered. Fifteen years in higher education left this person upset and demoralized, feeling isolated and with no support. The experiences all reflected the tone set by the president's leadership. Participant #8's remarked in closing, "Sure it is tough for women to rise in the ranks, but a woman can't lead without being a *monster*!"

> ...sure it is tough for women to rise in the ranks, but a woman can lead without being a MONSTER!

Participant # 4 also reflected on executive leaders as setting the tone. The office bully or "bad-boy" had been on staff for over years. Everyone knew about this his behavior, but nothing was done. Participant #4 on several occasions approached the president about how the bad boy was hampering communication, how his tantrums were disruptive to the mission and divided staff. Upon finding that the bad-boy bully was having tantrums and acting out, the president simply said "you two will have to fight it out..." Participant #4 at one point was supervising the bad-boy bully and was prepared to use progressive discipline and coaching to change his behavior or remove him. Again, when approaching the president for support, there was none. The president remarked, "We just won't go there..." As a result, the bully behavior continues, and still has an impact on that executive staff's functions.

Participant #5 worked for the same bully for over 15 years. He stated that the bully used covert tactics to unravel staff and challenge their confidence. No one stood up to the bully, who was the head of the department, because the bully repeatedly performed well by "bringing in the class."As the bully consistently generated revenue for the institution, her bullying antics were overlooked. Many simply saw the turnover in the office as staff "not being able to hack it..." The bullying behavior created cliques in the organization. Targets typically left within two years, and those in the "in group" adopted the bullying behaviors of the department head, and even did some of the bully's bidding. Participant #5 was specifically affected when he was told he shouldn't even try to advance his career with additional education; he wouldn't be promoted anyway. When he tried to leave, the bully blocked his job offer from another school. Since

> ...the organization adopted bullying tactics of the bully department head.

leaving that position, participant #5 received phone calls from other staff targets who were trying to complain formally about the bully. When targets complained to administration, it hurt remaining staff. If someone complained and then left, all those friends of the target who remained were subjected to additional bullying.

In his most recent position, Participant #5 witnessed how an administrative assistant was bullied by a group of faculty. The administrative assistant had started dating a faculty member. The faculty peers didn't like it and began to abuse her. Because this was a major research institution, the faculty members were kings; they got away with the behavior and the target had to transfer.

Participant #7 was concerned about the inappropriate ethical decisions forced on the office regarding financial aid. The bully didn't care about the regulations, despite constant reports and information from participant #7. The participant's duties were reassigned to cut this participant out of the information loop. The bullying treatment was known by administration, but nothing happened. The bully willingly and knowingly manipulated and forced decisions that federal regulations did not support.

> ...the bully willingly and knowingly manipulated and forced decisions that federal regulations did not support.

Theme #2: The Cost of Bad Behavior

Namie and Namie (2009) report that the United States spends $64 billion a year in dealing with workplace bullying. This data emerged from a study of corporate America by the Zogby International. European studies also document the cost of workplace bullying costing over €12 billion EU annually, with €1.55 billion lost in turnover, €9 billion lost through employee disengagement, and €3 billion lost to sick days and other absences (Ferris, 2009).

This segment extends this conversation to the fiscal loss in legal action, sick time, and disengagement in American higher education administration. In the face of statewide budget cuts, increasing tuition, and fluctuating enrollment, higher education cannot afford these costs simply to maintain a bully while also trying to stay focused on the herculean task of educating the no-child-left-behind generation of students matriculating to four-year schools.

Participant #6 reported that his school lost close to $1 million in sick time for people taking off to escape a hostile work environment. Another $2.5 million was lost in recruiting and retraining costs. Other costs included the cost to the school's reputation. Other organizations in the area would not work with this school because the school had a reputation for bad behavior and incivility. In turn, they lost a number of grant opportunities.

Participant #3 reported that the university did not take notice of the bully until two EEO complaints were filed against the school. The school was suffering depositions and the discovery process at the time of this interview. While the department's budget was $6 million, they had already spent $1.3 million in turnover, lawsuits, and sick time. These calculations did not include the projected cost to settle with the two complainants, or the money lost in fundraising because the university's reputation suffered in light of the lawsuits.

Participant #2 reported that she spent ten hours a week dealing with nasty emails, an aggressive staff and faculty just to defend herself from what she deemed organizational bullying. Assuming this employee made $45,000, her gross pay is $3750/mo. If she is spending 40 hours a month (25% of her time) staving off bullying, she spends $937.50 of salaried time on this issue, or $11,250 annually just to survive in this environment. This calculation doesn't include sick time and absenteeism that were reported in another section.

Imagine that the staff in general spent 25% of their time managing an aggressive, bullying environment. Two assistant directors at $45,000 =$90,000; three directors at $60,000 = $180,000 and two deans at $99,000= $198,000, with a total salary = $468,000 for the positions facing this behavior. This organization lost $117,000 over five years through staff disengaging from the organizational tasks to defending bullying behavior.

> They offered me a promotion. They can't pay me enough to get more involved here.

She also reported that she lost

three directors and two deans in five years. Each dean made $99,000 =$198,000. Recall that an organization loses 150% of a position salary when the person leaves. Therefore, in regard to deans' salaries, this organization had lost $297,000. This department had lost three directors in five years. Each director made approximately $60,000 = $180,000 as 150% of the salary is lost; this organization had lost $270,000 in five years. This participant was the second assistant director to leave. Using the same 150% salary loss calculation, assuming this position made $45,000 which equals $90,000 for two positions, $135,000 salary, *the salary loss alone over five years was $702,000.*

Participant #7 reported that the bullying led to turnover and eventually a lawsuit. This participant was called during the deposition process to speak about workplace bullying. While the case settled, the cost to defend any lawsuit to the point of summary judgment costs typically $100,000. Also, the turnover and employee disengagement were not calculated. Eventually, the bully, who was a provost, was fired by another executive bully. A safe guess would calculate over $500,000 in lawsuits, turnover costs, and disengagement.

Participant #4 reflected on the regular tantrums of a cabinet level bad-boy bully. The bully would get upset, yell, and throw things. After the outburst, he would walk out for half the day. This tantrum behavior occurred every two to three weeks while the president silently acquiesced. Assuming this bully made about $60,000, he spent about two days each month on tantrums and tantrum recovery. Two days a month for 12 months equals days; therefore, the organization lost about four and a half weeks of time nursing this tantrum behavior. About $5,500 or 9% of this salary was lost. This bully has been in place for over fifteen years. During that time, his organization has lost $82,500 in salary by overlooking tantrums. This doesn't include the time staff lost in recomposing themselves after witnessing another tantrum.

Theme #3: Coping with the bully's tactics

The nine participants in the qualitative section were ages 28 through 62. They represented different sectors and different organizational levels of higher education. Nonetheless, regardless of age or experience, all expressed disenchantment with toxic workplaces in higher education. Since the time of the interviews, four of the participants have left their positions, in part due to the aggression and hostility they faced or witnessed at work. Three other participants are actively looking to change positions in an effort to find a more healthy work environment.

Participant #2 described her experience as organizational bullying. She felt she had no support or protection from her vice president or human resources, as she was the constant target of a bullying unionized faculty. She remarked that she had been in meetings where she was yelled at, cursed at, and berated. Yet her dean and the vice president permitted the behavior from faculty. Human resources commented that it wasn't that department's area. Her

> ... I'm too young to lose my hair like this!

coping mechanisms included taking sick time and extended lunches. She would sit in her office with the door closed to avoid the constant barrage of complaints and aggressive behavior. In short, she disengaged to protect herself from a hostile environment. Despite her attempt to follow policy when she engaged with union staff, she didn't have the backing of her supervisors. She found herself desperately seeking a new job. Her health declined and resulted in hair loss and excessive sleeping. She often had ideation of walking off the job without giving two weeks' notice. Her experience was consistent with the previous three directors and an assistant director who worked in this office. Since this interview, she has since left the job.

Participant #1 and Participant #9 had very similar coping mechanisms. Both, regardless of religious affiliation, relied on meditation and a strong belief in a higher being to help them cope with a hostile environment. Both commented that they had to realize that it was the bully who had the problem. By relying on a deeper sense of self-worth and faith, they both weathered environments with bullies. Specifically, participant #1 commented, "I had to come to grips with the idea that *God* is running this. With that understanding, I know what goes around comes around..." In many ways, they both gave into the bully, gave him or her what they thought the bully wanted and didn't let their own feelings create a reaction to the bullying.

Participant # 3 was disappointed to find he had taken a job with a bully who was confident but not competent. The bully was a department head who would make unreasonable demands of participant #3.

Participant #3's budget was withheld while other staff members received budgets. The bully issued directives for participant #3 that ran counter to directives from the vice-

> I don't have to take this. I can LEAVE.

president (the bully reported to the vice president also). Even though HR told the bully not to admonish participant #3 for following the vice president's directives, the department head bully proceeded with an unfair reprimand of participant #3. The bully might have been confident, but lacked competence in managing staff or budgets. This resulted in two EEO complaints for the bully. At first, participant #3 had sleepless nights, panic attacks, and edginess related to stress. After a month, he realized that with his extensive experience, he could leave. He also took his complaints to the vice president. As participant #3's complaints coincided with the two EEO lawsuits, the administration did take notice and restructured the participant's duties, including reporting directly to the vice president.

Participant # 4 used avoidance to cope with the bad-boy behavior. Even though the bully was right down the hall, participant #4 would simply send emails when communication was necessary to avoid the tantrums. The rest of the staff also emailed the bully to avoid upsetting him. Participant #4 was concerned because even the president would use avoidance tactics instead of dealing with this bully. "Well, you know, we don't want to upset X." Participant #4 was not given the support to deal with the bully. Nor would the president stop the bullying behavior. Consequently, Participant #4's area worked in isolation, avoiding the bad-boy behavior.

Participant #5 made a point to work extra hard. He was exacting in his reporting and successful in his duties. He managed to stay away from office politics and not align himself with any one group. His focus on students and assisting students on campus helped him to ignore the aggression from his boss and her cronies. His colleagues who also were the target of the department head bully were stressed. Some fell into self-abusive behaviors such as alcoholism and overeating.

Participant #6 believed in facing the problem head on. He was a middle manager who quickly spotted bullying in his department. He studied the policies about collaboration, service to students, and team work. When the first bully challenged him in a memo, participant #6 called in the bully and stated, "It is my responsibility as department head to make sure we run efficiently, and that responsibility first falls on me. As the department head, I also have the responsibility of making sure staff is collaborating in the best interest of students..." The bullying behavior stopped. He commented, "Managers need to cut off the bullying behavior before it starts." Participant #6 unwaveringly applied policy to curtail bullying behaviors in his department. He realized that the bullies were acting out because the bullies had been mistreated previously. In turn, participant #6 was firm, but fair. He observed that it

> Managers need to cut off bullying behavior before it starts.

takes a certain personality to naturally know how to deal with bullies. The organization should provide training for managers and supervisors, and then support them in creating a healthy workplace.

Participant #7 stated that the bullying on the job led the participant to early retirement. The directives from the bully could have compromised the organization and the individuals who broke federal legislation. The participant believed there was no support because the bully was at the executive level. The participant's coping mechanism was to pursue early retirement.

Participant #8 felt overwhelmed by the bully. After meeting with the bully, the participant simply wanted to call the police as a result of the treatment. "She [the bully] just made me feel low...like I was worth nothing." Once participant #8 left the first organization, the bullying continued, with defamation in emails, notes, and blogs, to the participant's next organization. "I was devastated...why would anyone do this? She threatened my livelihood." Participant #8 had a meeting with her new human resources department once a defamatory note arrived from the bully at the previous institution. Participant #8 felt mildly depressed for a year, feeling the need to work three times as hard to disprove the unfair accusations in the note from the bully at her previous job. To this day, participant #8 remains hurt and disappointed. The participant is disillusioned with higher education, once believing

> It's not about the job. It's about the POWER people have over people.

that this sector would be a great place to work. Participant #8 closed the interview with, "It's not about the job…it's about the *power* people have over people." Despite years of success in higher education administration, participant #8 is leaving that field.

Theme #4: The Role of Human Resources and/ or EEO Office

With the exception of participant #9, who currently works in a place that explicitly embraces civility through policy and the modeled actions of the president, the other eight participants found human resources and or the EEO office to be ineffective in dealing with workplace bullying. Only two human resource offices responded positively once a complainant filed an external lawsuit. The qualitative findings reveal that even while the organization and human resources are aware of aggression and bullying coming from the powerful executive ranks, bullies tend to remain in place because they are seldom held accountable. These data reveal that bullies can stay in place 10–20 years and those subject to the bullying behavior continue to seek relief through transfer, resignation, and early retirement.

Participant #3 and Participant #7 both witnessed workplace bullying and were the targets of workplace bullying. In both cases, the bully was the boss who was unaware of federal or other national legislation that governed the area. Also in both cases, the aggression and arrogance of the bully brought the institution into question by external third parties through an audit or other external review. Human resources departments remained silent about the workplace aggression and bullying until the respective institutions were named in federal lawsuits about harassment and discrimination. While one organization eventually fired the bully and settled out of court with the complainant, the second organization faces two federal lawsuits because of the actions of the bully.

Participant #1 realized the human resources department was involved in transferring an administrative assistant who had complained about the executive bully boss. Participant #1 believed there was a for-

> "... hostility and the cover-up have become the new normal here..."

mal complaint internally to facilitate the transfer for the administrative assistant. However, after losing three administrative assistants, the bully executive boss was still in place and presumably not held accountable for bad behavior. Human resources perhaps had its hands tied, since the bully was on the highest level. His behavior had gone unchecked for years. The organization simply removed the target. In regard to bullying in the executive suite, participant #1 stated, "Hostility and the cover-up have become the new normal here."

Participant #2 had gone to the EEO officer several times with statistics and others about how she was treated unfairly and bullied by staff. While the faculty was unionized, she also argued that she faced bullying because of her race. She also pointed to the fact that the other assistant director and the directors were also black and also faced the same treatment. However, when a white male ran the office five years previously, the department didn't endure this heightened level of harassment from faculty. The EEO officer stated there was no case and referred participant #2 back to her dean, who did nothing to provide relief from this problem. Participant #2 also reflected on the lack of support from human resources when the previous assistant director had bullied her (when she served as a temp). Only when the previous bully (assistant director) literally cursed at a third-party vendor off campus, did human resources acknowledge there was even a problem of aggression and incivility within the department and toward the department. Participant #2 found human resources and the EEO office to be totally ineffective and spent close to eighteen months actively looking for a job.

Participant #5's remarks on human resources are similar to that of participant #1. While everyone knew who the bully was and how she operated, human resources and the executives turned their heads. There was no support for someone complaining about a toxic workplace. In fact those who complained faced retaliation, or their office buddies faced retaliation. The last person who stepped forward to human resources spent four years gathering information and support; but nothing much changed. He commented,

> "...we have all this sensitivity training, why isn't there training to stop bullying?

"We have all this sensitivity training, but there is no training on how to deal with bullying."

Participant #6 reflected on the ineffectiveness of human resources. His environment was heavily unionized. Therefore, the human resources department was overwhelmed with the constant grievances between union and staff. The human resources department couldn't penetrate the union, offer support to targets, or offer training on how to deal with bullying. Further, the Human Resources Department was rendered ineffective with the constant changes in the executive office, with eight presidents in years. They were always conducting a search or replacing someone who quit.

Theme #5: Impact on Services and Functions

Unlike the corporate sectors which reported 37% experiencing workplace bullying, this study reveals that 62% of people in higher education administration have witnessed or experienced bullying in the last 18 months. In addition to the personal and emotional cost to the target, and the fiscal cost to the organization, organizational functions and services are also affected by aggression and incivility. Five of the participants commented that aggression and bullying adversely affected operations. Three of the participants engaged in emotional labor, working extra hard under the pressure of a bully, yet still met objectives and goals.

Participant #5, Participant #7, Participant #8. While these three participants represented admissions, financial aid, and academic affairs,

> "...we worked extra hard to package students despite the stress..."

they also commented on their dedication to student services. In fact, focusing on student services and student achievement became an escape or coping mechanism to distract them from the aggression of a bully. Participant #5 stated, "It was hard working there, but I got a lot of joy out of helping students who would not have made it to our school without my help." Participant #7 remarked, "We worked extra hard to try to package students despite the stress..." Nonetheless, the antics of the bully also put participant #7's organization at risk for a federal audit. Participant #8 remarked, "I just focused on students. Sure, I couldn't be creative, but I made a point not to let them know how I was really feeling."

Participant #2 commented, "Students see how the faculty treats us. They see how secretaries treat each other. What motivation is there for students to act right? They act out and act belligerent too—the culture brings out the worst. Faculty gets mad that they have to work with students and do a poor job in working with students. Of course it affects students, when I am struggling to survive in this place; I have to make my well-being a priority. Unfortunately student concerns wind up second."

Participant # 3 reported that the bully withheld the budget as a bullying tactic. The budget was money used to provide academic support and tutoring to students. When the bully decided to withhold funds, the bully hurt students. Tutoring wasn't made available until a week before finals, when many of them couldn't fix poor grades. The bully also affected the development and fundraising arm. With all of the complaints and lawsuits, the reputation of the school was tarnished. Even though [the bully] was hired to raise money, "...he has not brought in one dime given all the other mess going on here..."

Participant #4 reflected on the bad-boy bully in the executive suite. While the bully didn't stop development functions, the bully was a distraction and hurt progress and innovation. Their department could maintain the status quo, but as far as developing new strategies and new ideas were concerned, "that couldn't happen. Innovation requires communication, and no one wanted to communicate with an unchecked bully. We just did the same thing, nothing new."

Participant # 6 reflected on how the constant bullying between union and non-union staff jeopardized student services. Not only did the frivolous use of grievances overwhelm human resources functions, it hampered service to students. While the organization was busy with meetings, yelling, cursing, and a range of infighting, student questions went unanswered, student concerns became secondary. Students suffer in an organization that is always fighting itself.

> "... students suffer in an organization that is always fighting itself. .."

Participant #9 reported on interdepartmental bullying between the bursar, admissions and the registrar.

The bullying between the directors resulted in a toxic environment, as their staff modeled the behavior. The bullying slowed process time and response time to students. Human resources worked with these three departments weekly to have them refocus on student services and find alternative ways to deal with frustration.

Chapter Five

Recommendations and Solutions

The Urgency in Higher Education

The findings reveal that aggression emerging from executive leadership is at the center of the workplace bullying problem in higher education. Findings also reveal that the problem is more pervasive in higher education than in general population. Throughout the organizational strata of higher education, leadership is a common thread either as the actor, or the enabler of bad behavior on campus. A target seeks leadership for relief after facing a bully. A manager consults with leadership when supervising a bully. Human resources follow leadership in response to a bully. And as documented, the bully is often from the ranks of leadership, in a position of power. Both quantitative and qualitative findings show that leadership can set the tone in cultivating an environment that will sustain bullying behavior or eradicate bullying behavior from campus.

In the midst of dealing with these internal dynamics, leadership in higher education is facing a series of challenges and criticisms. Fiscal challenges and demographic shifts create a need for change in a particularly stringent financial environment. Keeling and Hersch (2011) reflect on the quality of American higher education where many graduates received inflated grades, but can't handle complex problems, think, write on an advanced level, or help employers compete at the global level. They claim that "without higher learning, higher education is just a series of steps that lead to a degree; the receipt of which is evidence of nothing except completion of those steps" (para. 1, 2011).

The quality of higher education is strained by the Obama administration's stated goal for the United States to ascend from its rank of 16th to reclaim its global position as the international leader as the nation with the most college-educated adults. With the goal of increasing the number of college graduates by 60% by 2020 (from the current rate of 39% in 2012) tension is placed on all higher education sectors to produce another eight million graduates.

In contrast, in 2011, Bloomberg reported that the Obama administration has proposed budget cuts in higher education that would reduce support by $89 billion over the next ten years. Though such funds would be reallocated to the Elementary and Secondary Education Act and several competitive grant opportunities, higher education must innovate and compete for funding, instead of resting on its laurels awaiting fiscal support.

Fiscally, higher education is fighting constant budget cuts in the midst of rising tuition. Between 2008 and 2010, the average four-year tuition increased 15% amid budget cuts of 40% in many states such as Georgia, Arizona, California, and Pennsylvania. These cuts are laid over the increasing cost of higher education, which tripled in some cases. In response, some states have contemplated a tuition freeze, yet even this solution would have a deleterious impact on higher education.

With these budget cuts and challenges, higher education can't afford to lose valuable productivity to staff turnover and employee disengagement. As these findings reveal that bullying is more prevalent in higher education than in the general employment sector, a university with a staff of 2000 employees facing a rate of 62% being bullied (1240 employees enduring bullying) each wasting 187 hours toiling under the rule of a bully, loses close to $7.6 million in salary as a result of this employee disengagement. There is nothing about the aforementioned fiscal crises and expectations of higher education that suggests that any institution can afford this type of waste to ignore a bully.

These changes occur as the need for inclusion and access escalates.

In 2010, the *New York Times* announced that women were the official majority in the work force; and since 2000, women have been at least 57% of the college population. The "minority-majority" is emerging with the birth rate of non-whites outpacing that of white Americans. According to the United States Census, with minorities representing 37% of the population, four states, California, New Mexico, Texas, Hawaii, and the District of Columbia are "minority-majority states" with minorities expected to be the majority nationwide by 2040.

With these ensuing changes, American higher education must engage transformational leadership styles to motivate staff and invoke change; this leadership style relies on trust. "Trust is the essential link between the leader and the led, vital to people's job satisfaction and loyalty...and it is as fragile as it is precious; once damaged, it is nearly impossible to repair" (Evans, p. 287). In the midst of the aforementioned fiscal and demographic changes, leadership can galvanize an organization, or lead it simply to mediocrity and/or stagnation. To rise above mediocrity, transformation and innovation are critical elements for any organization, but neither can exist without trust for a leader with integrity. "Integrity is a fundamental consistency between one's values, goals, and actions. At the simplest level, it means standing for something, having a significant commitment, and exemplifying this commitment in your behavior" (p. 289). Therefore, consider the mission statements and goals set by many institutions of higher learning. Such statements include values of inclusion, collaboration, and cooperation. The fair assumption is that the leadership at the helm is aligned with the mission statements and values of the organization he or she leads. When leadership deviates from such mission values in action and behavior, not only is the leadership integrity questioned by followership, the inconsistency within the organization is exposed. The very integrity of the organization is in question.

Consistency in action and behavior should not only be embedded in the values of higher education for the purpose of educating students, but such consistency is a requirement to maintain a followership that looks to the executive leadership in the midst of this myriad of changes. Aggression and bullying at any level jeopardizes the mission and values of higher education; and further, executive bullying is incongruous with the stated values, especially when disenfranchised parties along gender, racial, and sexual orientation lines are disproportionately the targets of this aggression.

In converse, the quantitative and qualitative findings yielded models of success and civility in higher education. Healthy work environments not only included respect from colleagues, but also respect and support from supervisors and leadership. Study participants confirm that executive leadership who made a consistent commitment to the health of the organization, through policy, action, and behavior, created organizations with minimal aggression. These leaders, perhaps Level 5 leaders, who can lead with an iron will and disarming humility, cultivate trust in their vision. These leaders have the ability to "subjugate their own needs to the greater ambition of something large and more lasting than themselves. The Level 5 leader is not focused on "fame, fortune, power, and adulation, and so on. Work will ...be about what they can build create and contribute" (Collins, 2008, p. 112). Level 5 leadership is aligned with many of the values presented in these higher education mission statements.

Symbols, Missions and Accreditation

The proliferation of workplace bullying in higher education is beyond troubling in relation to organizational dynamics and its accreditation responsibilities. Organizations which have trusted leaders "...salted everywhere, [with] ordinary people doing extraordinary things ..." create a culture of innovation woven from a vision and value set that a staff can find inspiring. The executive leader can be a "living logo" or "human icon" who symbolizes and projects the organizational tenor by embodying the mission statement often espoused by the organization (Bolman and Deal, 2003, p. 254).

Accrediting bodies expect such symbolic mission statements which frame higher education to be more than window dressing and instead signal to constituents an accurate representation of the organizational vision and operation. Further, the organization's own mission statement is a central part of the accrediting process. The mission statement is held as a fundamental element as the mission is woven into the accreditation standards, operations, and academic expectation and evaluated through the lengthy accreditation process.

For example, the Southern Association of Colleges and Schools

Commission on Colleges Principles of Accreditation, 3.1 Institutional Mission states: "The mission statement is current and comprehensive, *accurately guides the institution's operations*, is periodically reviewed and updated, is approved by the governing board, and is communicated to the institution's constituencies" (2012, p. 25).

In standard 11 of the New England Association of Schools and Colleges Commission on Institutions, 11.1 states:

> The institution expects that members of its community, including the board, administration, faculty, staff, and students, will act responsibly and with integrity; and it systematically provides support in the pursuit thereof. Institutional leadership *fosters an atmosphere where issues of integrity can be openly considered,* and members of the institutional community understand and assume their responsibilities in the pursuit of integrity (2011, p.26).

The Middle States Characteristics of Excellence in Higher Education: Requirements of Affiliation and Standards for Accreditation also speaks to the importance of the mission which, delineates the scope of the institution, *explains the institution's character and individuality, and articulates values as appropriate.* The institution's basic purposes and characteristics, such as research or community service, should be addressed within the statement of mission. The mission may be accompanied by related statements, such as a statement of institutional philosophy (2006, p.1).

Therefore, mission statements from higher education which invoke values such as equity, fairness, collaboration, service, sensitivity, innovation, commitment, social justice and partnership, should form the consistent foundation for a culture of civility and trust, a culture which is mutually exclusive from bullying, incessant incivility, and aggression. The aforementioned findings of this study outline multiple instances of how bullying precipitates stress, ugly behavior, coercion, threats, manipulation and false accusations reported by the target. Further, respondents reported how such a culture leads to hair loss, denial, counseling, and suicide. Consequently, incongruence exists between what many organizations state as their mission, and the stressful day-to-day activity which repeatedly occur if a bully is freely roaming the courtyards of its campus.

For example, while there were several troubling remarks from study participants, one in particular drives the point home about leadership and aggression. The participant stated:

> I think the worst kind of bullying that I have witnessed occurred by a university president who yelled and screamed at a room full of faculty, staff, and administrators. This president threw papers down on the floor, showed aggressive body language, and actually yelled at the group. This kind of behavior is unbecoming of any university president, and is inexcusable (study participant, 2012).

This behavior from leadership doesn't reflect an open atmosphere, trust, integrity, collegiality or any sense of partnership which is typically discussed in a higher education organizational mission statement. Instead of fostering a cohesive environment in service to staff and students, this bullying behavior from leadership only drives all who witness such aggression back to their silos to watch the clock for quitting time. While toiling in their silos, staff members utilize emotional labor to rationalize what they witnessed, chatter among themselves about the disconcerting behavior they witnessed, or simply just shut down. In any case, the behavior and subsequent staff disengagement from the toxic environment is counterintuitive to the mission. Aggression and bullying erode the potentially inclusive and innovative culture of American higher education, which undercuts the expected values presented for accreditation.

When the symbolic values presented in the organizational mission statement do not align with the daily experiences of the staff subordinate to an aggressive boss, potentially an organization is not meeting the standards set for itself for accreditation. A bully can lead an organization to violate federal regulations and NCAA compliance standards. Bullying behavior can quickly lead an organization into discrimination and harassment charges as women, people of color and the LBGT community are disproportionately targeted. To invoke a phrase common to the NCAA, organizations that truly maintain "institutional control" stamp out bullying behavior through policy, training, and leadership who model civility. Those organizations which take this bullying trend lightly, not only lose millions of dollars, they come dangerously close to violating its self-proclaimed accreditation standards presented in its own mission statement.

Intersection of Harassment and Bullying

Bullying and harassment are synonyms. Both are belittling, demeaning treatment that escalates over time. The target is often left in a position where enduring the bad behavior is a condition of employment, especially when the bully is the boss. As these findings reveal, the targets tend to be from a perceived weaker position. Forty-seven percent of the women who responded to this study reported being the target of a bully. Fifty-five percent of African Americans in this WBAS study reported being the target of a bully. Bullying behavior can very quickly precipitate a Title VII lawsuit when the target is from a protected class defined by civil rights legislation.

In 2011, the EEOC reported 99,947 complaints—an all-time high. Thirty-five percent of the complaints were based on race; 28 % of the complaints were based on gender; and 23.5% of the complaints were based on age. As confirmed by a number of the open-ended responses, targets that also have membership in protected classes do have civil rights protections.

Further, as retaliation has evolved as the largest complaint area at 36% of the EEOC complaints, surpassing race for the first time since 1964, data show that employees are increasingly complaining about the negative responses from the boss or organization when the complainant exercises his or her civil rights. In short, a target participates in protected activities (files complaint, participates in an investigation), then faces adverse action on the job and has a second EEOC charge. Incivility after a complaint has been filed, yields retaliatory complaints by targets and also costs the organization hundreds of thousands of dollars.

With the intersection of harassment and bullying, and the disproportionate number of women and people of color reporting that they are targets of workplace bullying, organizations should include anti-bullying policies and training in its updates to managers and supervisors. While no one, regardless of Title VII status, should endure hostility on the job, the cost of litigation to defend such behavior should itself be a motivator for organizations to keep staff trained to avoid these practices that lead to costly legal action.

Recommendations and solutions: Organization, target, and bully

This study has revealed that workplace bullying in higher education is almost double the corporate rate of bullying. Further, the cause of bullying is a combination of power and lack of accountability. In turn, individuals are left with few options but to endure the problem and disengage from the environment, or leave the environment; as noted previously, both coping mechanisms for the target can cost colleges and universities millions in lost productivity, unfocussed staff, and legal action.

Based on the findings, this section will offer recommendations and solutions to create or maintain a healthy workplace in higher education. First, the discussion will consider organization wide solutions and provide an organizational model for success. Second, the recommendations will offer individual strategies for staff to find solace in the face of a bully boss. The individual recommendations will also offer a model of intervention for middle managers left supervising a bully without support from human resources or the boss. Third, this discussion will offer solutions for the bully. As many studies confirm, bullies tend to operate from a need to control, from learned behavior, from insecurity, or from a combination thereof. Ironically, they are killing the very productivity they are trying to cultivate with aggressive and bullying behavior.

Organizational Solutions
Stop the problem before it starts

Some popular commentary reflects on how the role of the human resource professional is given the task of protecting the organization, not the individual. Whether the complaint is regarding budgets, restructuring, or harassment, human resource staff members are typically charged with being the facilitator who shields the organization through tumultuous times. Considering this mission, the recruiter can indeed guard the organization at the point of recruitment and hiring as well. Aligning with the mission of serving and protecting the organization, recruiters can be a front line that can prevent the bully from invading a workplace environment.

Different workplace arenas tend to attract different personality types; for example, educational institutions and social organizations tend to attract those with "helping" personalities. With this in mind, recruiters and search committees can remain cognizant of the appropriate personalities for open positions, as well as learn some of the characteristics of a bully, ultimately avoiding recruiting them into an organization in the first place.

Human resources recruiters and search committees should be conscious of the impact a bully can have on any organization. As previously stated, bullying is a silent epidemic, with the bosses being the bullies 72% of the time. The Hollis WBAS study confirms that bullying is pervasive in higher education, costing colleges and universities billions of dollars.

People vote with their feet in organizations, not with their mouths, especially when they are under duress. Staff will not speak up against the newly recruited bully boss. As revealed, 16% of higher education respondents will have left a bully boss. When colleges and universities truly consider the cost of turnover, it should be motivation to stop the bullying problem before it starts, especially when most bullies are the boss. With 62% of respondents in higher education reporting that they are affected by bullying, and several reporting on the impact on student services, the negative effect on fundraising, and the legal risk of defending a bully, it is incumbent to stop the problem before it starts.

Typically innovative and high performing staff members are the first ones to leave. The mediocre staff members simply become disengaged and collect a paycheck in a toxic environment. Another scenario is the innovative staff member who is trapped in this position because of personal reasons (tuition remission, family illness), yet he or she also endures the bullying through disengagement. As bullying is the silent epidemic, draining organizations of already dwindling resources, the recruiting process can be the first step on a list of processes and interventions that can protect a healthy work environment.

Despite the public policy demand for higher education, college and university staff needs to be on guard for staff turnover due to bullying and incivility.

Recommendations for hiring and search committees in higher education:

1. Try to recognize potential bullies in the interview process. A bully is typically a good performer in the interview because he or she seeks to control the situation. However, interview procedures which include informal lunches or tours are opportunities to relax the recruited candidate and listen to his or her stories. Do they brag about "cracking the whip" or "cleaning house" in their last position? While restructuring might be necessary, a bully might take pleasure in asserting this control without empathizing with the impact on those staff members let go. Does the candidate make comments about being frustrated with

staff and brag about coercive tactics? Does the candidate ever show genuine empathy or concern for previous subordinates? Often a bully doesn't realize he or she is a bully, and will often talk about his or her behavior.

2. Maintain relationships that are a critical part of the process, and know what personalities can be successfully sustained in that culture. Knowing the culture can keep a naïve search committee from bringing a bully on campus. If the search committee knows the department it's recruiting for doesn't support shrinking violets, then don't bring in a weak personality who can end up being a target. Even a Harvard PhD cannot compensate for a personality that will not weather an aggressive department.

3. Know how the department or division receives aggressive and assertive personalities. If the organization thrives on a dynamic that is more like *Clash of the Titans*, bring in that assertive type. But if the organization is already facing high turnover, a shifting culture, a series of informal or formal complaints, or limited resources and RIFs (reduction in force) which makes for a nervous staff, recruiting a barracuda to "whip people into shape" might be the exact strategy to avoid.

4. Conduct a thorough vetting process and avoid the post-and-pray approach. Each leader should have a record of good behavior, turnover, complaints, or accolades. In the vetting process, determine if this shiny new star had longevity in the staff who reported to him. Ask objective questions about the candidate's

strategies to motivate previous staff. Did the strategies include respect or coercion? At the executive level, during the vetting process, request a 360 Evaluation report from the candidate's previous institution.

5. Engage in proper onboarding procedures. Assertive behavior relative to achieving objectives is good. Bullying away the productive people in the division is *bad*. Include anti-bullying policies in the onboarding process, and have such rules of civility discussed by the division head, even if via podcast or brief webinar. Stop the destructive behavior before it starts and protect the environment. Make it clear to the recruit throughout the hiring process and at the point of hire that incivility will not be tolerated.

6. Understand that workplace bullying can result in a complaint to human resources and/or an EEOC complaint. A savvy target of the bullying can find EEOC laws or a human resources policy to bring the situation to the forefront with a verbal or written complaint. These complaints often fall in categories of harassment, i.e., age, gender, or sexual. A harassment complaint, even an internal complaint, is costly and time consuming.

Work is tough enough as it is. Further, a new boss introduced into any environment will naturally invite questions or concerns from staff. If the new hire is properly vetted, and also coached that the work culture is one of civility that does not tolerate bullying, the campus is in a better position to reap the rewards of a productive organization, instead of constantly recruiting replacements for employees fleeing a toxic workplace.

Modified from ERE.net publication November 2011

Model for Organizational Success Healthy Workplace

The findings of this study and previous studies reveal that targets of bullying and witnesses of bullying are motivated to seek relief from the aggression they experience. Consistent with other studies, this study also corroborates previous findings that bullying often comes from leadership and that human resources seldom advocates for the target, leaving the target toiling in isolation, disengaging from organizational objectives, or leaving the organization. Those who are the targets and witnesses of workplace bullying utilize emotional labor and work two and three times as hard to serve students and external contacts. They suppress their stress and mask anxiety with a smile to get through the day. However, while the outward smile might keep the peace, the previous findings also reveal that innovation and progress can't be achieved in the midst of aggressive behavior. The emotional labor provides the semblance of composure, not collaborative innovation.

In contrast, the qualitative and quantitative findings also offer elements of success from leadership that can craft a healthy work environment in which employees can thrive. Such a healthy place emerges from the leader's consistent commitment to and alignment with institutional values. Executive leadership's integrity dissolves the need for staff's emotional labor and yields a healthy place to work.

Based on the qualitative and quantitative findings, a healthy workplace relies on an engaged and consistent executive leadership with integrity. As one respondent stated, "a good leader is needed—someone who won't play favorites." In sum, executive leadership can't tolerate aggression at *any* level, even from their closest colleagues. There should be an open environment that relies on trust and transparency. An executive leader needs to be visible and accessible, walk around on occasion and answer his/her own emails. The staff needs to know that leadership will intervene if aggressive behavior is present. Further, the leader needs to be sensitive to the power structures in the organization and not divulge the confidence of those strong enough to come forward with problems. Simultaneously, the leader would not undermine authority; but find ways to handle complaints quietly and discreetly. This is not to undercut the managers or supervisors, but as one of the participants stated, "self-policing is sometimes the best policing."

A culture of fairness and a cross section of representation can assist in managing aggression in staff and faculty ranks. A mediation committee of both faculty and staff can review cases and manage the environment. Instances of retaliation or misuse of policy and procedures to harass staff cannot be tolerated.

This model also includes an annual 360 Evaluation of managers, supervisors, and cabinet level staff. The president establishes a minimum standard for civility for his/her cabinet and executive staff. If someone consistently falls short, this leader would be coached to improvement. If the leader still exhibits aggressive behavior that stifles the organization, that leader would be removed, regardless of successes in other areas. As one participant stated, "civility would not be compromised for a million dollar grant..." While this might sound unreasonable given the economic times, the cost to higher education in relation to bullying behavior is unsustainable.

In addition to a transparent and accessible executive leadership, and the 360 Evaluations, leaders with healthy work environments often have workplace satisfaction surveys, which they should take seriously. In converse, gathering information and complaints in the name of a healthy workplace, then acting with apathy once results were tallied are actions that lack integrity with the staff and lose trust that is hard to regain. Other signs of trouble in a workplace include student complaints, high turnover, and the lack of internal transfers when positions opened in a particular department. Staff tacitly is aware of the aggressive personality, and often won't pursue even a higher paying position if it means being subjected to a bully manager.

Below is the leadership model for a healthy workplace. It relies on executive leadership developing trust and transparency. Consistent visibility is key; staff needs to trust and rely on leadership before there is a problem. The 360 evaluation is critical to garner objective feedback about the leadership styles of cabinet level and other high level leadership. Lastly, all staff members, even the executives, need to be held accountable for their actions. Often, the combination of power and the lack of accountability breeds bullying and aggression in higher education administration.

Figure 1: Organizational Leadership Model for a healthy workplace

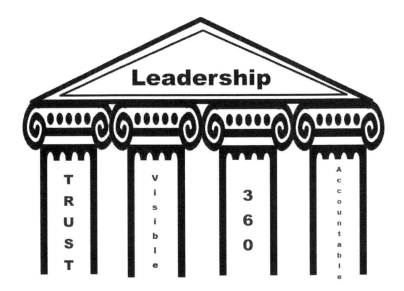

Organizational solutions summary:

1. Weed out bullies in the search process with 360 Evaluation.
2. Know the organizational culture and recruit leaders who lead by civility.
3. Engage in proper onboarding procedures for all staff with anti-bullying policies in place.
4. Maintain civil environment with 360 Evaluations of cabinet level positions.

5. Maintain accountability at all levels with civility as part of the formal evaluation structure.

6. Empower and encourage human resources to engage all levels of complaints.

7. Leadership must cultivate trust and transparency through access and visibility.

Individual/ Target Solutions

The organizational model of solutions provides a top-down approach to cultivating a healthy workplace and developing employee engagement. It requires consistent commitment from the executive office and surrounding cabinet positions. However, many respondents were from the middle management (assistant director, director, assistant or associate deans) who might have had some managerial or supervisory purview, but limited influence on a global scale across the organization. Nonetheless, respondents did offer a series of coping mechanisms that enabled them to withstand a bully and avoid some of the debilitating human costs which accompany high stress environments.

Some of the respondents reported high stress, hair loss, sleepless nights, alcoholism, and other self-abusive behaviors. Further, respondents commented that suicide was an option, along with walking off the job with no employment options, or trying to ignore the problem.

Figure 2: Self-Care Strategies

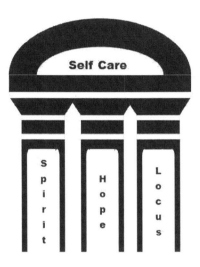

Others commented that a higher sense of self helped them withstand a bully. By having faith, they were able to be strong in the face of stress and aggression. The notion of a God, higher being, or something greater than oneself offered solace in the midst of bullying behavior or a toxic work environment. Several respondents commented on their faith that the bully would "get what he deserves," or "what goes around comes around." Belief in a higher being that exacts justice often was a common theme for those coping with a workplace bully. Such belief helped participants avoid the self-deprecating thoughts that often affect targets.

Coping respondents owned a locus of control with the realization they could leave or change the situation by changing jobs. Meditation and other self-care strategies such as embracing their success with students helped respondents to combat high blood pressure and anxiety. While many of these strategies are individual and personal, they all fit within the theoretical framework of emotional labor by staff to withstand a hostile work environment. In all cases reported by respondents, the ultimate relief came when the bully was removed from the environment or the target or witness left the environment.

Figure 3 Middle Management

Some middle managers reported success in managing a bully despite the presence of an overwhelmed human resources department or unstable executive leadership. While many organizations do have policy language regarding teamwork, collaboration, and service, a middle manager can build such policy language into objective performance standards to offset bullying. With such policy language, a middle manager should strive to curtail bullying behavior before it starts.

Lastly, a manager should be firm but fair. Often, targets are in the entry level positions of the middle level positions of an organization; the positions which don't have the power to defend against a bully. In turn, the manager is possibly working with a subordinate who has previously endured a bully boss. A middle manager who doesn't allow bullying behavior to flourish, but develops trust within the department can create a healthy workplace. Please note, that while a strong middle manager can make a difference in a department, without the support of leadership, or at least the latitude to make these changes in the performance, the middle manager would still be rendered a neutral figure at best in the attempt to quell bullying.

Individual/middle management solutions summary:

1. Engage in self-care, spiritual or otherwise.
2. Improve professional skills to remain professionally agile.
3. Create an identity for self that doesn't hinge on work.
4. Maintain locus of control, consider other employment options.
5. As manager, use policy language to curtail bullying behavior in the department.
6. Model civility, fairness, and respect for subordinates and colleagues.
7. Stop the problem before it starts. Speak with the bully quickly once bullying behavior is apparent.
8. Be firm yet fair in application of policy; don't play favorites.

Aggressor/Bully Solutions

The previous studies on workplace bullying report that bullies learn their behavior from past bosses, aggressive home environments, or other models that taught them that bullying was an acceptable method to motivate or control people. Further, as the studies confirm, most bullying comes from leadership, where the formal power structure resides.

For all leadership, the goal is a productive and innovative staff that can solve problems and create solutions with limited resources. Creativity and innovation seldom emerge from toxic environments; in fact, staff will take the innovation and creativity with them by fleeing the organization, or turning inward to self. To the response of a bully boss, one middle manager commented, "I won't give her my pearls...I won't offer my ideas." Ironically, while bullying stems from a need to control and produce, bullying actually promotes mediocrity.

Further, guidance for the bully is not about absolving staff of its responsibility to maintain standards, or meet objectively defined goals. Often it is not the message that is communicated to staff which creates the problem; it is how the messages come across that becomes a problem.

Therefore, instead of engaging in bullying tactics, consider the overall goal for the department or division. If someone needs coaching or discipline, the leader should be clear and objective in setting goals and include the staff member while designing these expectations. The staff member might not be in a position to set goals, but should be included in a civil conversation about changing objectives and allowed to offer insight into how those goals can be met.

Figure 4 Bully Intervention

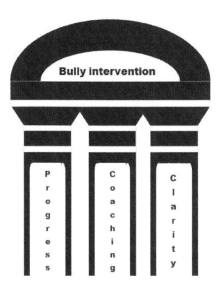

If the bully just has an aggressive personality learned from previous experiences, executive coaching is an excellent solution. Coaching can be a confidential method to refine management strategies. Unlike psychological counseling, which encourages clients to develop their solutions, coaching will offer concrete assignments and specific objectives for the client. Executive coaching can cost $250 to $450 an hour. This cost pales in comparison to the millions of dollars lost in disengaged staff or turnover because subordinates can't produce in a toxic work environment.

Also, leadership can seek mentors at other institutions and through networking to *unlearn* bullying behaviors. The cultivation of mutual respect, civility, and meaningful rewards systems are essential for higher education staff. Higher education, like most sectors in 2012, is a knowledge based culture that requires formal education of its employees. The days of because-I-said-so management are gone. Staff is motivated and inspired, not so much directed and demeaned into submission.

Further, leadership can review the trends in their own departments. High turnover is nothing to be shrugged off with "we wanted all those people to leave anyway." Turnover is costly and can even lead to the loss of staff positions in the midst of a budget crisis. If plum positions open but few internal people apply, that is a sure sign that this department is perceived as having problems.

Aggressor/bully solutions summary:

1. Track productivity and turnover.
2. Review internal transfer patterns.
3. Seek executive coaching.
4. Communicate clearly and fairly with staff.
5. Seek mentors to help the bullies *unlearn* bullying behavior.
6. Initiate a 360 Evaluation for yourself and management in the department.

Recommendations for Future Study

While this was a groundbreaking work that surveyed over 175 four-year colleges and universities, recommendations for future study would include strategies for more input from diverse populations, younger staff, and executive staff. A nationwide study would encourage a more diverse population to give feedback.

1. Develop strategy, perhaps through an executive organization, to cultivate more executive response. Many of the respondents to this study were from the middle of the organization. The insight from the executives in the qualitative interviews offered insight for the need to include more executive voices.

2. The current sample of this study had a majority of respondents from ages 40–49 and 50–59. A younger pool would also include a more diverse population. The shifting demographics show that the United States is quickly approaching a "minority-majority" status which comes from the young population under. Therefore, a future recommendation would include a younger and more diverse population which would be more representative of the demographic shifts in the United States.

3. Develop an in-depth study in regard to administrative and faculty unions. Some of the open-ended quantitative answers and some of the qualitative interviews pointed to an abuse of power from unions in regard to bullying. This statement doesn't

advance the idea that staff should not enjoy union protections. In retrospect, note that one participant specifically spoke about her highly unionized environment, but was clear about how her president managed civility specifically from the top down. Nonetheless, as those in the union seek union protection to ward off abuses from within the organization, the power of the union can unfairly harm those in such an organization who don't enjoy union protections if the organization doesn't operate with the modeled bounds of civility. As a result, this study reports that unionized staff, if unchecked, at times wields power over those outside of union protection through aggression and mobbing behaviors.

Afterword

With over twenty years in higher education, and serving in several cabinet level positions, I understand first-hand how an engaged and innovative staff in higher education can move an organization forward, better serve students, and maintain its position as a pillar in the community. Inspired action from positive engagement can emerge from all corners of the organization, the faculty ranks, development, athletics, and the executive ranks, and assist any organization in meeting its own expectations. However, the demise of such engagement can also lurk in the shadows of administrative behavior. Early in my career, I witnessed directly the internal destruction to staff morale, enduring a toxic environment. In contrast, I have led healthy environments based on civility and collaboration to cultivate solutions, even in the face of budget deficits. Inspired employee engagement has been proven to bridge the gap.

Until this publication, workplace bullying in higher education administration has been discussed in hushed tones and at times ignored to maintain organizational appearances. The hope is these findings will assist leaders at all levels of higher education. The findings of this study should be a wake-up call to the costly practice of accepting bully behavior. Therefore, the solutions can help higher education leaders maintain healthy work environments for those entrusted with educating the next generation of Americans.

Dr. Jeffrey Holmes, 2012

References

Allport, G. (1979). *The nature of prejudice*. Addison-Wesley Publishing Company, Reading, MA.

Bliss, W. (2012). Cost of employee turnover. *Small Business Advisor*. Retrieved August 11, 2012 Retrieved from http://www.isquare.com/turnover.cfm

Bolman, L. and Deal, T. (2003). *Reframing organizations: artistry, choice and leadership*. Jossey Bass, San Francisco, CA.

Collins, J, (2008). Level 5 leadership: the triumph of humility and fierce resolve. *Business Leadership*. Jossey Bass, San Francisco, CA.

Commission on Institutions of Higher Education. New England Association of Schools and Colleges. (2011). *Standards of accreditations*, Bedford, MA.

Constanti, P and Gibbs, P. (2004). Higher education teachers and emotional labour. *The International Journal of Educational Management, 18* 4–5.

Davenport, N., Schwartz R., and Elliot, G. (1999). *Mobbing: emotional abuse in the American workplace*. Civil Society Publishing, Collins, IA.

Deholm, A. (2011). Survey reveals extent of bullying. *The Herald Glasgow [UK]*, 22.

EEOC. (2012). Prohibited employment practices. Retrieved August 15, 2012 from www.eeoc. gov/laws/practices/index.cfm

Einarsen, S., Hogel, H., Zapf, D., and Cooper, C. (2011). *Bullying and harassment in the workplace*. CRC Press, Boca Raton, FL.

Evans, R.(2000). The Authentic Leader. *Educational Leadership*. Jossey Bass. San Francisco, CA.

European Agency for Safety and Health at Work. (2002).*FACTS 23 Bullying at work*. ISSN 1681-2123. Retrieved June 15, 2012 from http://osha.europa.eu/en/publications/factsheets/23/.

European Agency for Safety and Health at Work. (2002). *Stress.* Retrieved June 15, 2012 from http://osha.europa.eu/en/topics/stress.

Ferris, P. (2009). The role of the consulting psychologist in the prevention, detection, and correction of bullying and mobbing in the workplace. *Consultating Psychology Journal Practice and Research, 61*(3), 169-189. doi:10. 1037/a0016783

Hochschild, A. (2003). *The managed heart: commercialization of human feeling*. University of California Press, Los Angeles, CA.

HR & Diversity Management LTD. (2010). *Bullying in the Workplace: The size of the problem*. National Bully Hotline. Retrieved June 15, 2012 from www.nationalbullyinghelpline.co.uk.

Hunt, S. (2008). Warning: chronic bullying is hazardous to the academy's health. *The Times Higher Education Supplement* 26. Retrieved from http://search.proquest. com/docview761045035 ?accountid=35812

Jurnak, M. (2010). The cost of losing good employees. *New Hampshire Business Review, 32(1).*

Keashly, L. and Neuman, J. (2010). Faculty experience with bullying in higher education: causes, consequences, and management. *Administrative Theory and Praxis.32* (1). 48-70.

Keelan, E. (2000). Bully for you. *Accountancy*. 125, 56.

Keeling. R. and Herch, R. (2001). *We're losing our minds. Rethinking American higher education*. Palgrave MacMillan, New York.

Middle States Commission on Higher Education. (2006). *Characteristics of excellent in higher education*, Philadelphia, PA.

Namie, G., and Namie, R. (2009). *The bully at work: what you can do to stop the hurt and reclaim your dignity on the job*. Sourcebooks, Napersville, IL.

Pearson, C. (1999). Rude managers make for bad business. *Workforce*, 78, 18.

Query, T. and Hanely, G. (2010) Recognizing and managing risks associated with workplace bullying. *CPCU Journal, July*, 1-8.

Quine, L. (1999). Workplace bullying in NHS community trust: staff questionnaire. *British Medical Journal, 318*, 288-232.

Rayner, C. (1998). Bullying at work survey report- UNISO Retrieved June 20, 2012 from www. bullyinginstitutes.org.home/tcvd/bb/res

Rayner, C. (2006). What does bullying cost your business. *People Management*. Retrieved Aug 2011 from www.peoplemanagement. co.uk.

Southern Association of Colleges and Schools Commission on Colleges. (2012). *The principles of accreditation: foundations for quality enhancement*, Decatur, GA.

Thomas, M. (2005). Bullying among support staff in a higher education institution. *Health Education, 105*(4), 273-288.

Thomson, A. (2010). Workplace bullying rife in the second, union claims. *The Times Educational Supplement*. 4891. Retrieved February 1, 2012 from http://search.proquest. com/docview/580 112603?accountid=35812

Tomassini, J. (2012). US drops in global innovation rankings. *Education Week*. Retrieved August 12, 2012. Blogs. edweek. org/edweek/ marketplacek12/2012/07/US-drops-in-globe-innovation-rankings.html.

West, C. (1994). *Race matters*. Beacon Press, Boston.

Other works

Cassell, M. (2011). Bullying in academic: *prevalent significant and incessant. Contemporary issues in education research,* 4.5, 33-44.

Cavaiola, A., and Lavender, N. (2000). *Toxic coworkers: How to deal with dysfunctional people on the job.* New Harbinger Publications Inc., Oakland, CA.

Daniel, T. (2009). *Stop bullying at work: strategies and tools for HR and legal professionals.* Society of Human Resource Management, Alexandria, VA.

Frost, P. (2003). *Toxic emotions at work.* Harvard Business School Publishing, Cambridge.

Heames, J. and Harvey, M. (2006). Workplace bullying: A cross-level assessment. *Management Decisions. 44*(9), 1214-123.

Lubit, R. (2004). *Coping with toxic managers, subordinates and other difficult people.* Prentice Hall, Upper Saddle River, NJ.

McNair, F. (1997). Abuse: an employee killer. Options exist to correct bad situations short of quitting out right. *Edmond Journal of Management, E 10,* Retrieved from http://search.proquest.com/docview/252446273?accountid=35812

Osif, B. (2010). Workplace bully. *Library Leadership and Management, 24* (4), 206-212.

Veincentotzs, M. (2009). *How organizations empower bully bosses: a criminal in the workplace.* Aventine Press, San Diego.

Pearson, C. and Porath, C. (2009). *The cost of bad behavior: how incivility is damaging your business and what to do about it.* Portfolio Hardcover, New York.

Index

About the Author

D R. LEAH P. HOLLIS is a noted educator, researcher, and lecturer. She has an exemplary career in higher education administration and has held senior leadership and faculty posts. Dr. Hollis has taught at Northeastern University, the New Jersey Institute of Technology, and Rutgers University. Dr. Hollis received her Bachelor of Arts degree from Rutgers University and her Master of Arts degree from the University of Pittsburgh. She received her Doctorate of Education in Administration, Training, and Policy Studies from Boston University, as a Martin Luther King, Jr. Fellow. Also, Dr. Hollis continued her professional training at Harvard University through the Graduate School of Education, Higher Education Management Development Program.

She also earned certification in Project Management and Executive Leadership at Stanford University and Cornell University respectively. Further, she has earned certifications in EEO Law/Affirmative Action and Conflict Resolution and Investigation from the American Association for Affirmative Action. Dr. Hollis has served as a diversity trainer for Northeastern University and she speaks regionally and nationally on such topics as race, gender, ethnicity, equality, and access. Her first book, *Unequal Opportunity: Fired without Cause, Filing with the EEOC,* based on qualitative interviews of women who endured workplace discrimination, was published in 2011. For more information on Dr. Hollis and her consulting group, Patricia Berkly LLC, visit, www.diversitytrainingconsultants.com.

SPONSORS for:
BULLY IN THE IVORY TOWER

Special thanks to the **Bruce Haselrig Group**
for their support of this important venture.

Anonymous donors

Antoine Bernard

Carol Mohamed

Clara Wajngurt, Ph.D.

Jessica Hrabovsky

Karen Swift

Michael Stanford

Professor Claudia B. Jones

Robert Hollis

Roxanne Maldonodo

Velia Rincon

Victoria King

Made in the USA
Lexington, KY
30 January 2014